# Agile Project Management Using Team Foundation Server 2015

Joachim Rossberg

*Agile Project Management Using Team Foundation Server 2015*

Joachim Rossberg
Goteborg, Sweden

ISBN-13 (pbk): 978-1-4842-1869-3          ISBN-13 (electronic): 978-1-4842-1870-9
DOI 10.1007/978-1-4842-1870-9

Library of Congress Control Number: 2016940378

Managing Director: Welmoed Spahr
Lead Editor: James DeWolf
Development Editor: Douglas Pundick
Technical Reviewer: Fabio Claudio Ferracchiati
Editorial Board: Steve Anglin, Pramila Balen, Louise Corrigan, Jim DeWolf, Jonathan Gennick,
    Robert Hutchinson, Celestin Suresh John, James Markham, Susan McDermott, Matthew Moodie,
    Jeffrey Pepper, Douglas Pundick, Ben Renow-Clarke, Gwenan Spearing
Coordinating Editor: Melissa Maldonado
Copy Editor: Keia Endsley
Compositor: SPi Global
Indexer: SPi Global
Artist: SPi Global

Distributed to the book trade worldwide by Springer Science+Business Media New York, 233 Spring Street, 6th Floor, New York, NY 10013. Phone 1-800-SPRINGER, fax (201) 348-4505, e-mail orders-ny@springer-sbm.com, or visit www.springer.com. Apress Media, LLC is a California LLC and the sole member (owner) is Springer Science + Business Media Finance Inc (SSBM Finance Inc). SSBM Finance Inc is a Delaware corporation.

For information on translations, please e-mail rights@apress.com, or visit www.apress.com.

Apress and friends of ED books may be purchased in bulk for academic, corporate, or promotional use. eBook versions and licenses are also available for most titles. For more information, reference our Special Bulk Sales–eBook Licensing web page at www.apress.com/bulk-sales.

Any source code or other supplementary material referenced by the author in this text is available to readers at www.apress.com. For detailed information about how to locate your book's source code, go to www.apress.com/source-code/.

Printed on acid-free paper

*This one is for Amelie, Eddie, and Karin.*

# Contents at a Glance

About the Author ................................................................. xiii

About the Technical Reviewer .................................................. xv

Acknowledgments ................................................................ xvii

Introduction ...................................................................... xix

■Chapter 1: Introduction to Application Lifecycle Management ............... 1

■Chapter 2: An Overview of TFS ............................................... 19

■Chapter 3: Introduction to Scrum and Agile Concepts ...................... 37

■Chapter 4: Work Items and Process Templates ............................... 65

■Chapter 5: Customizing the Process Template in TFS ........................ 87

■Chapter 6: Agile Practices in TFS .......................................... 117

■Chapter 7: Metrics in Agile Projects ....................................... 131

■Chapter 8: Agile Project Management in TFS ................................. 147

Index ............................................................................. 187

# Contents

About the Author ................................................................................................ xiii

About the Technical Reviewer ............................................................................ xv

Acknowledgments .............................................................................................. xvii

Introduction ...................................................................................................... xix

■Chapter 1: Introduction to Application Lifecycle Management ........................... 1

Aspects of the ALM Process ........................................................................................ 1

Four Ways of Looking at ALM ....................................................................................... 4

    The SDLC View ......................................................................................................................... 5

    The Service Management or Operations View ........................................................................... 6

    The Application Portfolio Management View .............................................................................. 6

    The Unified View ....................................................................................................................... 7

Three Pillars of Traditional Application Lifecycle Management .................................... 7

    Traceability .............................................................................................................................. 8

    Automation of High-Level Processes ........................................................................................ 8

    Visibility into the Progress of Development Efforts .................................................................... 9

A Brief History of ALM Tools and Concepts ................................................................. 9

    Application Lifecycle Management 1.0 ...................................................................................... 10

    Application Lifecycle Management 2.0 ...................................................................................... 12

    Application Lifecycle Management 2.0+ .................................................................................... 15

DevOps ...................................................................................................................... 17

Summary .................................................................................................................... 18

■**Chapter 2: An Overview of TFS** ................................................................ **19**

Application Lifecycle Management Overview ........................................... 19

Team Foundation Server Overview ......................................................... 20

Team Foundation Server............................................................................... 20

Process Template ......................................................................................... 22

Visual Studio 2015 Editions ......................................................................... 23

TFS Web........................................................................................................ 24

Microsoft Office ............................................................................................ 24

Integrated Development Environment (IDE) Integration ................................ 24

Traceability ............................................................................................. 25

The TFS Work Item Tracking System ............................................................. 25

Visibility.................................................................................................. 30

Collaboration ......................................................................................... 31

Work Items for Collaboration........................................................................ 32

The Gap Between IT and Business ................................................................. 33

Use of One Role-Based Tool ................................................................... 34

Extensibility............................................................................................ 34

Differences Between TFS and VSTS ........................................................ 34

Summary................................................................................................. 35

■**Chapter 3: Introduction to Scrum and Agile Concepts** ........................... **37**

The Scrum Framework............................................................................. 37

Empirical Process Control............................................................................. 38

Complexity in Projects.................................................................................. 39

What Scrum Is .............................................................................................. 40

Roles in Scrum ............................................................................................. 42

The Scrum Process........................................................................................ 43

Definition of Done ........................................................................................ 46

Agile Requirements and Estimation .............................................................. 48

During the Sprint ........................................................................................... 51

Kanban ............................................................................................................... 53

    Start With What You Do Now..................................................................................... 54

    Agree to Pursue Incremental, Evolutionary Change ................................................. 54

    Respect the Current Process, Roles, Responsibilities, and Titles ........................... 54

    The Five Core Properties .......................................................................................... 54

    Common Models Used to Understand Work in Kanban ............................................ 57

Extreme Programming ...................................................................................... 58

Scaling Scrum .................................................................................................. 59

SAFe ................................................................................................................. 59

Scaled Professional Scrum (SPS) ..................................................................... 61

How Agile Maps to ALM .................................................................................... 63

    Agile Captures Task-Based Work .............................................................................. 63

    Increased Frequency of Inspection........................................................................... 63

    Many Tools Collect Much Information........................................................................ 63

    Test Artifacts Are Important ...................................................................................... 64

    Agile Teams Plan Frequently.................................................................................... 64

Summary ........................................................................................................... 64

Chapter 4: Work Items and Process Templates ...................................... 65

ALM Revisited.................................................................................................... 65

Traceability ....................................................................................................... 66

    The TFS Work Item Tracking System ........................................................................ 66

    Work Items ............................................................................................................... 67

The Process in TFS ........................................................................................... 76

    Agile, CMMI, and Scrum.......................................................................................... 76

Summary ........................................................................................................... 85

■**Chapter 5: Customizing the Process Template in TFS** .......................................... **87**

Process Customization ................................................................................................ 87

    Modifying the Process Template In TFS On-Premise .......................................................... 87

    Common Adaptations of the Process Template ................................................................. 90

    Modifying the Process Template in Visual Studio Team Services ...................................... 102

Summary ................................................................................................................. 115

■**Chapter 6: Agile Practices in TFS** ....................................................................... **117**

Agile Testing ........................................................................................................... 117

Acceptance Criteria ................................................................................................ 118

Evolving Tests ......................................................................................................... 119

    Clients for Managing Tests ............................................................................................ 120

Test-Driven Development ........................................................................................ 122

Working with Automated Tests ................................................................................ 123

Continuous Integration ........................................................................................... 123

    Why Continuous Integration? ........................................................................................ 124

Continuous Delivery ................................................................................................ 126

Coding Standard ..................................................................................................... 127

Refactoring ............................................................................................................. 128

Pair Programming ................................................................................................... 128

Summary ................................................................................................................. 129

■**Chapter 7: Metrics in Agile Projects** .................................................................... **131**

Project-Management Metrics .................................................................................. 131

    Agile Metrics ................................................................................................................ 131

Metrics for Architecture, Analysis and Design ........................................................ 136

Metrics for Developer Practices .............................................................................. 136

    Code Coverage ............................................................................................................. 137

    Code Metrics ................................................................................................................ 137

    Compiler Warnings ....................................................................................................... 137

    Code Analysis Warnings ................................................................................................ 138

Metrics for Software Testing ................................................................. 138

Example Reports............................................................................. 138

Metrics for Release Management ........................................................ 141

Sample Reports ............................................................................. 141

Using Charts to Monitor Metrics........................................................ 143

Summary ......................................................................................... 145

Chapter 8: Agile Project Management in TFS ....................................... 147

Case Study ..................................................................................... 147

Company Background ..................................................................... 147

The Pilot Project ........................................................................... 148

Scrum Process ................................................................................ 148

TFS/VSTS Web Portal..................................................................... 149

Charts and Queries ........................................................................ 150

Project Startup Phase..................................................................... 152

PO Sets Off to Work ....................................................................... 152

Building the Initial Team ................................................................. 153

Creating New Teams ....................................................................... 154

The Backlog and Team Structure for the Fabrikam Pilot ..................... 157

Building the Teams ......................................................................... 158

Adding Team Members.................................................................... 159

Managing VSTS Groups, Teams, and User's Permission......................... 161

Managing Alerts .............................................................................. 162

Requirements ................................................................................ 163

Building the Backlog....................................................................... 164

Definition of Done (DoD) ................................................................ 166

Estimation..................................................................................... 167

Risk Assessment ........................................................................... 168

Refining the Backlog ...................................................................... 169

Initial Velocity ............................................................................................. 169

    Available Time............................................................................................... 169

    Capacity Planning in TFS ............................................................................... 170

    Initial Sprint Planning ................................................................................... 171

    Updating Backlog and PBI ............................................................................. 172

    Forecast in TFS ............................................................................................. 173

Release Planning .......................................................................................... 175

    Epics ............................................................................................................ 175

    Estimated Time Plan ..................................................................................... 176

Estimated Project Cost ................................................................................. 176

Scrum Meetings During the Sprint ................................................................ 176

    Sprint Planning ............................................................................................. 177

    Daily Stand-Up ............................................................................................. 182

    Retrieving Data from TFS/VSTS ...................................................................... 183

    Backlog Refinement ...................................................................................... 185

    Sprint Review ............................................................................................... 185

    Sprint Retrospective ...................................................................................... 186

Summary ...................................................................................................... 186

Index ............................................................................................................ 187

# About the Author

**Joachim Rossberg** has worked as an IT consultant since 1998. He is primarily a product owner and project manager, but has an extensive history as a system developer/designer. Joachim is a certified Scrum Master and Product Owner. He has also demonstrated his technical background with various achievements over the years, including MCSD, MCDBA, MCSA, and MCSE. His specialties include agile project management, ALM processes, and Team Foundation Server. Joachim now works for Solidify in Gothenburg, Sweden.

# About the Technical Reviewer

**Fabio Claudio Ferracchiati** is a senior consultant and a senior analyst/developer using Microsoft technologies. He works for Blu Arancio (`www.bluarancio.com`). He is a Microsoft Certified Solution Developer for .NET, a Microsoft Certified Application Developer for .NET, a Microsoft Certified Professional, and a prolific author and technical reviewer. Over the past 10 years, he's written articles for Italian and international magazines and coauthored more than 10 books on a variety of computer topics.

# Acknowledgments

Thanks to everyone who helped me through this book. No one mentioned, no one forgotten. Except for one person I want to thank especially. Mathias Olausson, my coworker and manager, who wrote a great book on Continuous Delivery with Visual Studio ALM 2015 for Apress. Check it out at http://www.amazon.com/Continuous-Delivery-Visual-Studio-2015/dp/1484212738/ref=sr_1_1?ie=UTF8&qid=1461920928&sr=8-1&keywords=mathias+olausson.

# Introduction

This book covers agile project management using Team Foundation Server and Visual Studio Team Services. It provides many examples from both of these versions of TFS. However, this is not a hands-on book, instead it is aimed at providing useful information especially for product owners so that they know what TFS is and how it can be used in an agile world.

■ ■ ■

# CHAPTER 1

# Introduction to Application Lifecycle Management

What do you think about when you hear the term *Application Lifecycle Management (ALM)*? During a seminar tour in 2005 in Sweden, presenting on Microsoft Visual Studio Team System, we asked people what ALM was and whether they cared about it. To our surprise, many people equated ALM with operations and maintenance. This is still often the case when we visit companies, although more people today are aware of the term.

Was that your answer as well? Does ALM include more than just operations? Yes, it does. ALM is the thread that ties the development lifecycle together. It involves all the steps necessary to coordinate development lifecycle activities. Operations are just one part of the ALM process. Other elements range from requirements gathering to more technical things like the build and deploy processes.

## Aspects of the ALM Process

All software development includes various steps performed by people playing specific roles. There are many different roles, or disciplines, in the ALM process, and we define some of them in this section. (The process could include more roles, but we focus on the primary ones.)

Look at Figure 1-1, which illustrates ALM and some of its aspects. You can see the flow from the birth of an application, when the business need first arises, to when the business need no longer exists and the application dies. Once the thought of a new application (or system) is born, many organizations do some portfolio rationalization. This means you discuss whether an existing system can handle the need or whether a new system has to be developed. If a new system must be built, you enter the *software development lifecycle (SDLC)* and develop the system, test it, and deploy the system into operation. This is the point at which you do a handover so that operations can maintain and refine the system. Once in production, the system (hopefully) delivers the intended business value until retirement. While in operation, the system usually is updated or undergoes bug fixes; at such times, *change requests (CRs)* are written. For each CR, you go through the same process again.

© Joachim Rossberg 2016
J. Rossberg, *Agile Project Management using Team Foundation Server 2015*,
DOI 10.1007/978-1-4842-1870-9_1

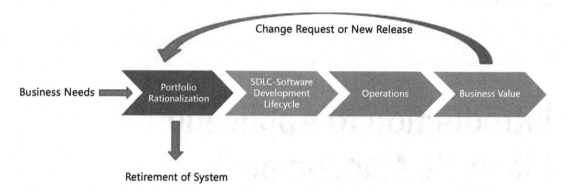

**Figure 1-1.** *The Application Lifecycle Management process*

It's essential to understand that all business software development is a team effort. The roles require collaboration in order to deliver business value to the organization. If you don't have this collaboration, the value of the system most likely will be considerably lower than it could be. One step up from the project level, it's also important to have collaboration between all roles involved in the ALM process, so that you perform this process in the most optimal way.

The roles in the ALM process include, but aren't limited to, the following:

- *Stakeholders:* Stakeholders are usually the people who either pay for the project or have decision-making rights about what to build. We like to also include end users in this group so not only management has a stake in a project.

- *Business manager:* Somebody has to decide that a development activity is going to start. After initial analysis of the business needs, a business manager decides to initiate a project to develop an application or system that will deliver the expected business value. A business manager, for instance, must be involved in the approval process for a new suggested project, including portfolio rationalization, before the company makes a decision to go ahead. IT managers are also part of this process, of course, because IT staff will probably be involved in the project's development and deployment into the infrastructure.

- *Project manager, product owner, or Scrum master:* Suitable individuals are selected to fill these roles, and they set to work on the project after the company decides to go ahead with the project. Ideally, these people continue leading the project all the way through, so that you have continuity in project management.

- *Project Management Office (PMO) decision makers:* These individuals are also involved in planning, because a new project may change or expand the company's portfolio.

- *Business analyst:* After requirements collection starts, the business analyst has much to do. Usually, initial requirements are gathered when the business need arises, but the real work often begins after portfolio rationalization. A business analyst is responsible for analyzing the business needs and requirements of the stakeholders, to help identify business problems and propose solutions. Within the system's development lifecycle, the business analyst typically performs a collaborative function between the business side of an enterprise and the providers of services to the enterprise.

- *Architect:* The architect draws an initial picture of the solution. We don't go into detail here, because Chapter 4 does that. But briefly, the architect draws the blueprint of the system, and the system designers or engineers use this blueprint. The blueprint includes the level of freedom necessary in the system: scalability, hardware replacement, new user interfaces, and so on. The architect must consider all these issues.

- *User experience (UX) design team:* UX design should be a core deliverable and not something you leave to the developers to handle. Unfortunately, it's often overlooked; it should be given more consideration. It's important to have close collaboration between the UX team (which could be just one person) and the development team. The best solution is obviously to have a UX expert on the development team throughout the project, but sometimes that isn't possible. The UX design is important in making sure users can perceive the value of the system. You can write the best business logic in the world, but if the UX is badly designed, users probably won't think the system is any good.

- *Database administrators (DBAs):* Almost every business system or application uses a database in some way. DBAs can make your databases run like lightning with good up-time, so it's essential to use their expertise in any project involving a database. Be nice to them; they can give you lots of tips about how to make a smarter system. Alas for DBAs, developers handle this work more and more frequently. This means developers are expected to have vertical knowledge and not just focus on coding.

- *Developers:* "Developers, developers, developers!" as Microsoft CEO Steve Ballmer shouted in a famous video. And who can blame him? These are the people working their magic to realize the system by using the architecture blueprint drawn from the requirements. Moreover, developers modify or extend the code when change requests come in.

- *Testers:* I'd rather not see testing as a separate activity. Don't get me wrong, it's a role, but testing is something you should consider from the first time you write down a requirement and continue doing during the whole process. Testers and test managers help you secure quality, but modern development practices include testing by developers as well. For instance, in Test Driven Development (TDD), developers write tests that can be automated and run at build time or as part of checking in to version control.

- *Operations and maintenance staff:* When an application or system is finished, it's handed over to operations. The operations staff takes care of it until it retires, often with the help of the original developers, who come in to do bug fixes and new upgrades. Don't forget to involve these people early in the process, at the point when the initial architecture is considered, and keep them involved with the project until everything is done. They can provide great input about what can and can't be done within the company infrastructure. So, operations is just one part—although an important one—of ALM.

All project efforts are done collaboratively. No role can act separately from the others if you're to succeed with any project. It's essential for everybody involved to have a collaborative mindset and to have the business value as their primary focus at every phase of the project.

If you're part of an agile development process, such as a Scrum project, you might have only three roles: product owner, Scrum master, and team members. This doesn't mean the roles just described don't apply, though! They're all essential in most projects; it's just that in an agile project, you may not be labeled a developer or an architect. Rather, you're a team member, and you and your co-members share responsibility for the work you're doing. We go deeper into the agile world later in the book (see Chapter 4).

# Four Ways of Looking at ALM

ALM is the glue that ties together the roles we just discussed and the activities they perform. Let's consider four ways of looking at ALM (see Figure 1-2). We've chosen these four because we've seen this separation in many of the organizations we've worked with or spoken to:

- *Software development lifecycle (SDLC) view:* This is perhaps the most common way of looking at ALM, because development has "owned" management of the application lifecycle for a long time. This could be an effect of the gap between the business side and the IT side in most organizations, and IT has taken the lead.

- *Service management or operations view:* Operations have also been (in our experience) unfortunately separated from IT development. This has resulted in operations having its own view of ALM and the problems in this area.

- *Application Portfolio Management (APM) view:* Again, perhaps because of the gap between business and IT, we've seen many organizations with a portfolio ALM strategy in which IT development is only one small part. From a business view, the focus has been on how to handle the portfolio and not on the entire ALM process.

- *Unified view:* Fortunately, some organizations focus on the entire ALM process by including all three of the preceding views. This is the only way to take control over, and optimize, ALM. For a CIO, it's essential to have this view all the time; otherwise, things can easily get out of hand.

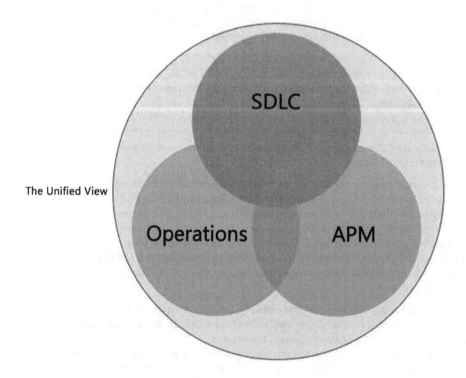

*Figure 1-2. The four ways of looking at ALM*

Let's look at these four views in more detail, starting with the SDLC view.

# The SDLC View

Let's consider ALM from an SDLC perspective first. In Figure 1-3, you can see the different phases of a typical development project and the roles most frequently involved. Keep in mind that this is a simplified view for the sake of this discussion. We've also tried to fit in the different roles from the ALM process, presented earlier.

| Analysis | Management Decision | Initial Requirement | Initial Architecture | Development | Delivery |
|---|---|---|---|---|---|
| Stakeholder | | Project manager<br>Business Analysis | Architect | Developr<br>UI Design<br>DBA | Operations |

*Figure 1-3.* *A simplified view of a typical development project*

First, somebody comes up with an idea based analyzing the business needs: "Hey, wouldn't it be great if we had a system that could help us do this (whatever the idea is)?" It can also be the other way around; the idea comes first, and the business value is evaluated based on the idea.

An analysis or feasibility study is performed, costs are estimated, and (hopefully) a decision is made by IT and business management to start an IT project. A project manager (PM) is selected to be responsible for the project; the PM begins gathering requirements with the help of business analysts, PMO decision makers, users, or others affected. The PM also starts planning the project in as much detail as possible at this moment.

When that is done, the architect begins looking at how to realize the new system, and the initial design is chosen. The initial design is evaluated and updated based on what happens during the project and how requirements change throughout the project. Development beings, including work performed by developers, user interface (UI) designers, and DBAs (and anyone else not mentioned here but important for the project).

Testing is, at least for us, something done all along the way—from requirements specification to delivered code—so it doesn't get a separate box in Figure 1-3. We include acceptance testing by end users or stakeholders in the Development box. After the system has gone through acceptance testing, it's delivered to operations for use in the organization. Of course, the process doesn't end here. This cycle is generally repeated over and over as new versions are rolled out and bug fixes are implemented.

What ALM does in this development process is support the coordination of all development lifecycle activities by doing the following:

- Making sure you have processes that span these activities.

- Managing the relationships between development project artifacts used or produced by these activities (in other words, providing traceability). These artifacts include UI mockups done at requirements gathering, source code, executable code, build scripts, test plans, and so on.

- Reporting on the progress of the development effort as a whole so you have transparency for everyone regarding project advancement.

As you can see, ALM doesn't support a specific activity: its purpose is to keep all activities in sync. It does this so you can focus on delivering systems that meet the needs and requirements of the business. By having an ALM process that helps you synchronize your development activities, you can more easily determine if any activity is underperforming and thus take corrective actions.

## The Service Management or Operations View

From a service management or operations view, you can look at ALM as in this quote from *ITIL Application Management* by the Office of Government Commerce in the United Kingdom (TSO, 2002): ALM "focuses on the activities that are involved with the deployment, operation, support, and optimization of the application. The main objective is to ensure that the application, once built and deployed, can meet the service level that has been defined for it."

When you see ALM from this perspective, it focuses on the life of an application or system in a production environment. If, in the SDLC view, the development lifecycle starts with the decision to go ahead with a project, here it starts with deployment into the production environment. Once deployed, the application is operated by the operations crew. They handle bug fixes and change requests, and they also pat the application on its back (so to speak) to make it feel good and run smoothly.

This is a healthy way of looking at ALM in our opinion: Development and operations are two pieces of ALM, cooperating to manage the entire ALM process. You should consider both pieces from the beginning when planning a development project; you can't have one without the other.

## The Application Portfolio Management View

In the APM view of ALM, you see the application as a product managed as part of a portfolio of products. APM is a subset of Project Portfolio Management (PPM)[1]. Figure 1-4 illustrates this process.

This view comes from the Project Management Institute (PMI). Managing resources and the projects they work on is very important for any organization. In Figure 1-4, you can see that the product lifecycle starts with a business plan—the product is an application or system that is one part of the business plan. An idea for an application is turned into a project and carried out through the project phases until it's turned over to operations as a finished product.

When business requirements change or a new release (an upgrade in Figure 1-4) is required for some other reason, the project lifecycle starts again, and a new release is handed over to operations. After a while (maybe years), the system or application is discarded (this is called *divestment*, the opposite of investment). This view doesn't specifically speak about the operations part or the development part of the process but should instead be seen in the light of APM.

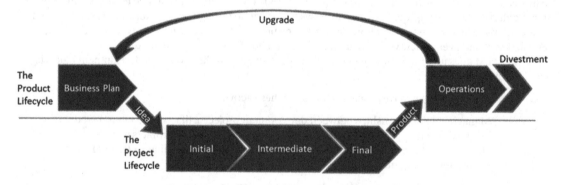

*Figure 1-4. The APM view of ALM*

---

[1]The PMI is the world's leading not-for-profit professional membership association for the project, program, and portfolio management profession. Read more at **www.pmi.org**.

## The Unified View

Finally, there is a unified view of ALM. In this case, an effort is made to align the previous views with the business. Here you do as the CIO would do: you focus on the business needs, not on separate views. You do this to improve the capacity and agility of a project from beginning to end. Figure 1-5 shows an overview of the unified ALM view of a business.

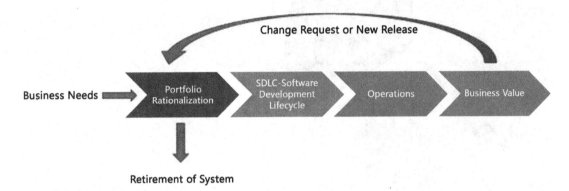

**Figure 1-5.** *The unified view takes into consideration all three views previously mentioned*

You probably recognize this figure from Figure 1-1. We want to stress that with the unified view, you need to consider all aspects from the birth to the death of an application or a system, hence the circle around the figure.

# Three Pillars of Traditional Application Lifecycle Management

Let's now look at some important pillars of ALM that are independent of the view you take; see Figure 1-6. These pillars were introduced by Forrester Research.[2]

---

[2]Dave West, "The Time Is Right For ALM 2.0+," October 19, 2010, Forrester Research, www.forrester.com/The+Time+Is+Right+For+ALM+20/fulltext/-/E-RES56832?objectid=RES56832.

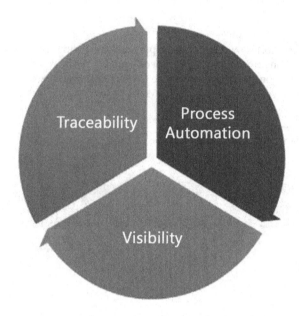

*Figure 1-6.* *The three pillars of ALM*

The following sections go over these pillars in greater detail, starting with traceability.

## Traceability

Some customers we've seen have stopped performing upgrades on systems running in production because their companies had poor or no traceability in their systems. For these customers, it was far too expensive to do upgrades because of the unexpected effects even a small change could have. The companies had no way of knowing which original requirements were implemented where in the applications. The effect was that a small change in one part of the code might affect another part, which would come as a surprise because poor traceability meant they had no way of seeing the code connection in advance. One customers claimed (as we've heard in discussions with many other customers) that traceability can be a major cost driver in any enterprise if not done correctly.

There must be a way to trace requirements all the way to delivered code—through architect models, design models, build scripts, unit tests, test cases, and so on—not only to make it easier to go back into the system when implementing bug fixes, but also to demonstrate that the system has delivered the things the business wanted.

You also need traceability in order to achieve internal as well as external compliance with rules and regulations. If you develop applications for the medical industry, for example, you must comply with FDA regulations. You also need traceability when change requests come in so you know where you updated the system and in which version you performed the update.

## Automation of High-Level Processes

The next pillar of ALM automating high-level processes. All organizations have processes in some way or the other. In some organizations there are no written down, formal processes, but they still have processes. For example, approval processes control handoffs between the analysis and design or build steps, or between deployment and testing. Much of this is done manually in many projects, and ALM stresses the importance of automating these tasks for a more effective and less time-consuming process. Having an automated process also decreases the error rate compared to handling the process manually.

## Visibility into the Progress of Development Efforts

The third and last pillar of ALM is providing visibility into the progress of development efforts. Many managers and stakeholders have limited visibility into the progress of development projects. The visibility they have often comes from steering-group meetings, during which the project manager reviews the current situation. Some would argue that this limitation is good, but if you want an effective process, you must ensure visibility.

Other interest groups, such as project members, also have limited visibility of the entire project despite being part of the project. This is often due to the fact that reporting is difficult and can involve a lot of manual work. Daily status reports take too much time and effort to produce, especially when you have information in many repositories.

# A Brief History of ALM Tools and Concepts

You can resolve the three pillars of ALM manually if you want to, without using tools or automation. (ALM isn't a new process description, even though Microsoft, IBM, HP, Atlassian, and the other big software houses are pushing ALM to drive sales of their respective ALM solutions.) You can, for instance, continue to use Excel spreadsheets or, like one of our most dedicated agile colleagues, use sticky notes and a pad of paper to track requirements through use cases/scenarios, test cases, code, build, and so on, to delivered code. It works, but this process takes a lot of time and requires much manual effort. With constant pressure to keep costs down, you need to make tracking requirements more effective.

Of course, project members can simplify the process by keeping reporting to the bare minimum. With a good tool or set of tools, you can cut time (and thus costs) and effort, and still get the required traceability you want in your projects. The same goes for reporting and other activities. Tools can, in our opinion, help you be more effective and also help you automate much of the ALM process into the tool(s).

Having the process built directly into your tools helps prevent the people involved from missing important steps by simplifying things. For instance, the agile friend we mentioned could definitely gain much from this, and he is looking into Microsoft Team Foundation Server (TFS) to see how that set of tools can help him and his teams be more productive. Process automation and the use of tools to support and simplify daily jobs are great because they can keep you from making unnecessary mistakes.

Serena Software Inc. is one supplier of ALM tools, and the company has interesting insight into ALM and related concepts. According to Serena Software, there are eight ALM concepts:[3]

- *Modeling:* Software modeling

- *Issue management:* Keeping track of incoming issues during development and operations

- *Design:* Designing the system or application

- *Construction:* Developing the system or application

- *Production monitoring:* The work of the operations staff

---

[3]Kelly A. Shaw, PhD, "Application Lifecycle Management for the Enterprise," Serena Software Inc., April 2007, www.serena.com/docs/repository/company/serena_alm_2.0_for_t.pdf.

- *Build:* Building the executable code

- *Test:* Testing the software

- *Release management:* Planning application releases

In order to synchronize these efforts, according to Serena Software, you need tools that span them and that help you automate and simplify the following activities. If you look closely, you can see that these activities compare to ALM 2.0+, which we discuss shortly:

- Reporting

- Traceability

- Policies

- Procedures

- Processes

- Collaboration

Imagine the Herculean task of keeping all those things in order manually. It's impossible, if you want to get things right and keep an eye on the project's status. Projects today seem to be going better because the number of failed projects is decreasing. Much of this progress is, according to Michael Azoff at the Butler Group,[4] the result of "major changes in software development: open source software projects; the Agile development movement; and advances in tooling, notably Application Lifecycle Management (ALM) tools." Some of these results have also been confirmed by later research, such as that by Scott W. Ambler at Ambysoft.[5] Now you understand why finding tools and development processes to help you with ALM is important.

There is increasing awareness of the ALM process among enterprises. We see this among our customers. ALM is much more important now than it was only five years ago.

# Application Lifecycle Management 1.0

Forrester Research has introduced some very useful concepts for ALM,[6] including different versions of ALM and ALM tools. This section looks at how Forrester defined ALM 1.0 and then continues to the latest version, ALM 2.0+.

As software has become more and more complex, role specialization has increased in IT organizations. This has led to functional silos in different areas (roles), such as project management, business analysis, architecture, development, database administration, testing, and so on. As you may recall from the beginning of this chapter, you can see this in the ALM circle. Having these silos in a company isn't a problem, but having them without any positive interaction between them is an issue.

There is always a problem when you build impenetrable walls around you. ALM vendors have driven this wall construction, because most of their tools historically have been developed for particular silos. For example, if you look at build-management tools, they have supported the build silo (naturally) but have little or no interaction with test and validation tools (which is strange because the first thing that usually happens in a test cycle is the build). This occurs despite the fact that interaction between roles can generate obvious synergies with great potential. You need to synchronize the ALM process to make the role-centric processes part of the overall process. This might sound obvious, but it hasn't happened until recently.

---

[4]Michael Azoff, "Application Lifecycle Management Making a Difference," February 2007, *Enterprise Networks and Services, OpinionWire.*
[5]"2011 IT Project Success Rates Survey Results," www.ambysoft.com/surveys/success2011.html.
[6]West, "The Time Is Right For ALM 2.0+."

Instead of having complete integration between the roles or disciplines mentioned at the start of the chapter and the tools they use, there has been point-to-point integration—for example, a development tool is slightly integrated with a testing tool (or, probably the other way around). Each tool uses its own data repository, so traceability and reporting are hard to handle in such an environment (see Figure 1-7).

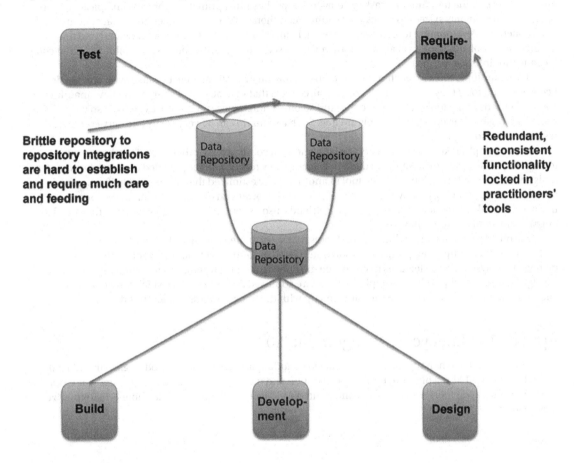

*Figure 1-7.* *ALM 1.0*

This point-to-point integration makes the ALM process fragile and expensive. However, this isn't just a characteristic of ALM 1.0—it's true for all integrations. Imagine that one tool is updated or replaced: the integration may break, and new solutions have to be found to get it working again. This scenario can be a reality if, for example, old functions in the updated or replaced tool are obsolete and the new tool doesn't support backward compatibility. What would happen if Microsoft Word (to take an easy example) suddenly stopped supporting older Word files? There would be more or less a riot among users until the situation was fixed. This can be hard to solve even with integration between two tools. What if you have a more complex situation, including several tools? We've seen projects using six or seven tools during development, creating a fragile solution when new versions are released.

Tools have also been centered on one discipline. In real life, a project member working as a developer, for instance, often also acts as an architect or a tester. Because the people in each of these disciplines have their own tool (or set of tools), the project member must use several tools and switch between them. It could also be that the task system is separated from the rest of the tools, so to start working on a task, a developer must first retrieve the task from the task system—perhaps they must print it out, or copy and paste it, then open the requirements system to check the requirement, then look at the architecture in that system, and finally open the development tool to begin working. Hopefully the testing tools are integrated into the development tool; otherwise, yet another tool must be used. All this switching costs valuable time that could be better put into solving the task.

Having multiple tools for each project member is obviously costly as well, because everyone needs licenses for the tools they use. Even with open source tools that may be free of charge, you have maintenance costs, adaptions of the tools, developer costs, and so on. Maintenance can be very expensive, so you shouldn't forget this even when the tools are free. Such a scenario can be very costly and very complex. It's probably also fragile.

As an example, take two co-workers at a large medical company in Gothenburg. They have a mix of tools in their everyday work. We asked them to estimate how much time they needed to switch between tools and transfer information from one tool to another. They estimated that they spend half an hour to an hour each day syncing their work. Usually they're on the lower end of that scale, but in the long run all the switching takes a lot of time and money. Our friends also experience problems whenever they need to upgrade any of the systems they use.

One other problem with traditional ALM tools that's worth mentioning is that vendors often add features: for example, adapting a test tool to support issue and defect management. In the issue-management system, some features may have been added to support testing. Because neither tool has enough features to support both disciplines, users are confused and don't know which tool to use. In the end, most purchase both, just to be safe, and end up with the integration issues described earlier.

## Application Lifecycle Management 2.0

Let's look at what the emerging tools and practices (including processes and methodologies) in ALM 2.0 try to do for you. ALM is a platform for the coordination and management of development activities, not a collection of lifecycle tools with locked-in and limited ALM features. Figure 1-8 and Table 1-1 summarize these efforts.

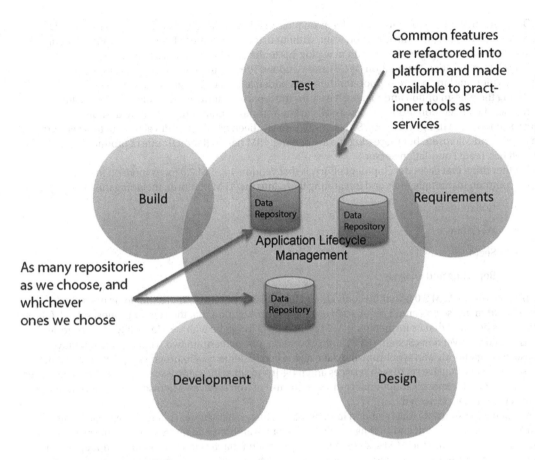

*Figure 1-8.* *ALM 2.0*

*Table 1-1.* *Characteristics of ALM 2.0*

| Characteristic | Benefit |
|---|---|
| Practitioner tools assembled from plug-ins | Customers pay only for the features they need.<br>Practitioners find the features they need more quickly. |
| Common services available across practitioner tools | Easier for vendors to deploy enhancements to shared features.<br>Ensures correspondence of activities across practitioner tools. |
| Repository neutral | No need to migrate old assets.<br>Better support for cross-platform development. |
| Use of open integration standards | Easier for customers and partners to build deeper integrations with third-party tools. |
| Microprocesses and macroprocesses governed by an externalized workflow | Processes are versionable assets.<br>Processes can share common components. |

One of the first things you can see is a focus on plug-ins. This means from one tool, you can add the features you need to perform the tasks you want, without using several tools! If you've used Visual Studio, you've seen that it's straightforward to add new plug-ins to the development environment. Support for Windows Communication Foundation (WCF) and Windows Presentation Services, for example, was available as plug-ins long before support for them was added as part of Visual Studio 2008.

Having the plug-in option and making it easy for third-party vendors to write plug-ins for the tool greatly eases the integration problems discussed earlier. You can almost compare this to a smorgasbord, where you choose the things you want. So far this has mostly been adopted by development tool vendors such as IBM and Microsoft, but more plug-ins are coming. IBM has its Rational suite of products, and Microsoft has Team Foundation Server.

Another thing that eases development efforts is that vendors in ALM 2.0 focus more on identifying features common to multiple tools and integrating them into the ALM platform, including the following:

- Collaboration

- Workflow

- Security

- Reporting and analysis

Another goal of ALM 2.0 is that the tools should be repository neutral. There should be not a single repository but many, so you aren't required to use the storage solution that the vendor proposes. IBM, for example, has declared that its forthcoming ALM solution will integrate with a wide variety of repositories, such as Concurrent Versions System (CVS) and Subversion, just to mention two. This approach removes the obstacle of gathering and synchronizing data, giving you easier access to progress reports, and so on. Microsoft uses an extensive set of web services and plug-ins to solve the same issue. It has one storage center (SQL Server); but by exposing functionality through the use of web services, Microsoft has made it fairly easy to connect to other tools as well.

An open and extensible ALM solution lets companies integrate their own choice of repository into the ALM tool. Both Microsoft and IBM have solutions—data warehouse adapters—that enable existing repositories to be tied into the ALM system. A large organization that has invested in tools and repositories probably doesn't want to change everything for a new ALM system; hence it's essential to have this option. Any way you choose to solve the problem will work, giving you the possibility of having a well-connected and synchronized ALM platform.

Furthermore, ALM 2.0 focuses on being built on an open integration standard. As you know, Microsoft exposes TFS functionality through web services. This isn't publicly documented and isn't supported by Microsoft, however, so you need to do some research and go through some trial and error in order to get it working. This way, you can support new tools as long as they also use an open standard, and third-party vendors have the option of writing cool and productive tools.

Process support built in to the ALM platform is another important feature. By this we mean having automated support for the ALM process built right into the tool(s). You can, for instance, have the development process (RUP, Scrum, XP, and so on) automated in the tool, reminding you of each step in the process so you don't miss creating and maintaining any deliverables or checkpoints.

In the case of TFS, this support includes having the document structure, including templates for all documents, available on the project web site as soon as a new TFS project is created. You can also imagine a tool with built-in capabilities that help you with requirements gathering and specification. For instance, you can add requirements and specs to the tool and have them transformed into tasks that are assigned to the correct role without your having to do this manually.

An organization isn't likely to scrap a way of working just because the new ALM tool says it can't import that specific process. It has often invested a lot of money into developing that process, and the organization won't want to spend the same amount again to learn a new one. With ALM 2.0, it's possible to store the ALM process in a readable format such as XML.

The benefits include the fact that the process can be easily modified, version controlled, and reported on. The ALM platform can then import the process and execute the application development process descriptions in it. Microsoft, for example, uses XML to store the development process in TFS. The process XML file describes the entire ALM process, and many different process files can coexist. This means you can choose which process template you want to base your project on when creating a new project.

As you saw earlier, it's important for an enterprise to have control over its project portfolio, to better allocate and control resources. So far, none of the ALM vendors has integrated this support into the ALM platform. There may be good reasons, though. For instance, although portfolio management may require data from ALM, the reverse probably isn't the case. The good thing is that having a standards-based platform makes integration with PPM tools much easier.

## Application Lifecycle Management 2.0+

So far, not all ALM 2.0 features have been implemented by most of the major ALM tool vendors. There are various reasons. One is that it isn't easy for any company to move to a single integrated suite, no matter how promising the benefits may appear. Making such a switch means changing the way you work in your development processes and maybe even throughout your company. Companies have invested in tools and practices, and spending time and money on a new platform can require considerably more investment.

For Microsoft-focused development organizations, the switch might not be as difficult, however—at least, not for the developers. They already use Visual Studio, SharePoint, and many other applications in their daily life, and the switch isn't that great. But Microsoft isn't the only platform out there, and competitors like IBM, Serena, and HP still have some work to do to convince the market.

In addition, repository-neutral standards and services haven't evolved over time. Microsoft, for instance, still relies on SQL Server as a repository and hasn't built much support for other databases or services. The same goes for most competition to TFS.

---

■ **Note** Virtually all vendors use ALM tools to lock in customers to as many of their products as possible—especially *expensive* major strategic products like RDBMS. After all, these companies live mostly on license sales.

---

The growth of agile development and project management in recent years has also changed the way ALM must support development teams and organizations. There has been a clear change from requirements specs to backlog-driven work, and the tooling you use needs to support this change.

It becomes critical for ALM tools to support agile practices such as build-and-test automation. TDD is being used with increasing frequency, and more and more developers require their tools to support this way of working. If the tools don't do that, they're of little use to an agile organization. Microsoft has taken the agile way of working to heart in the development of TFS; this book shows you all you need to know about TFS's support for agile practices.

There has also been a move from traditional project management toward an agile view where the product owner and Scrum master require support from the tools. *Backlog grooming* (the art of grooming requirements in the agile world), agile estimation and planning, and reporting—important to these roles—need to be integrated into the overall ALM solution.

The connection between operations and maintenance also becomes more and more important. ALM tools should integrate with the tools used by these parts of the organization.

In the report "The Time Is Right for ALM 2.0+," Forrester research presented the ALM 2.0+ concept, illustrated in Figure 1-9.[7] This report extended traditional ALM with what Forrester called ALM 2.0+. Traditional ALM covers traceability, reporting, and process automation, as you've seen. Forrester envisions the future of ALM also including collaboration and work planning.

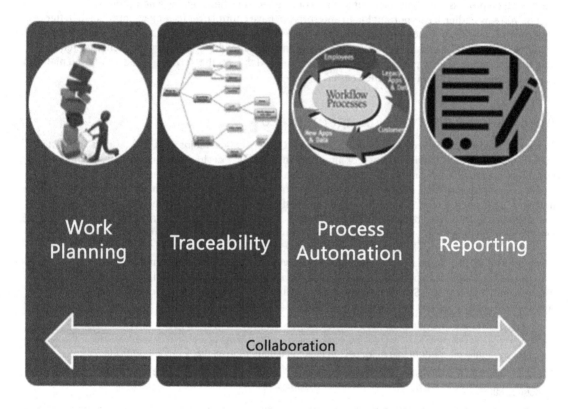

***Figure 1-9.*** *Future ALM, according to Forrester Research*

These concepts are essential throughout the rest of this book: A chapter is dedicated to each one except for traceability and visibility that are combined into one chapter since they are closely related. The book's focus is on ALM 2.0+, but it includes some other older concepts as well. We've already looked at the first three cornerstones, but let's briefly examine the two new ones introduced in ALM 2.0+:

- *Work planning:* In this concept Forrester includes planning functions, such as defining tasks and allocating them to resources. These planning functions shouldn't replace the strategic planning functions that enterprise architecture and portfolio-management tools provide. Instead, they help you execute and provide feedback on those strategic plans. Integration of planning into ALM 2.0+ helps you follow up on projects so you can obtain estimates and effort statistics, which are essential to all projects.

---

[7]West, "The Time Is Right For ALM 2.0+."

- *Collaboration*: This is essential. ALM 2.0+ tools must support the distributed development environment that exists in many organizations. The tools must help team members work effectively—sharing, collaborating, and interacting as if they were collocated. The tools should also do this without adding complexity to the work environment.

We take a closer look at these topics further down the road. But before that, we examine a new topic on the horizon: DevOps. It's important because it has the potential to solve many ALM problems.

# DevOps

The last couple of years have seen the concept of DevOps emerge. In our view, DevOps is close to, or even the same as, the unified view of ALM presented earlier in the chapter. One big difference compared to a more traditional approach is that DevOps brings development and operations staff closer not just in thought but also physically. Because they're all part of the DevOps team, there is no handover from one part to the other—team members work together to deliver business value through continuous development and operations. Figure 1-10 shows how Microsoft looks at DevOps.

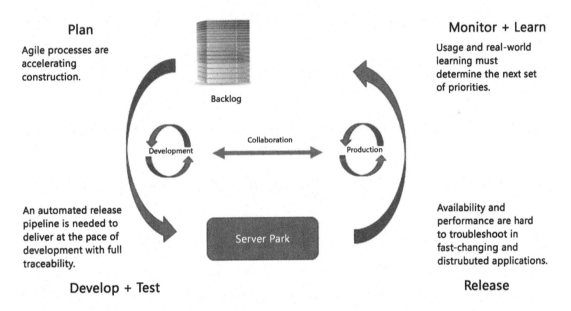

**Figure 1-10.** *DevOps according to Microsoft*

DevOps isn't a method on its own; instead, it uses known agile methods and processes like Kanban and Scrum, which are popular in many IT organizations. Basically, these are project-management methods based on agile concepts and are used for development (mostly Scrum) and operations (mostly Kanban). The key concepts are continuous development, continuous integration, and continuous operations. What is important is working with small changes instead of large releases (which minimizes risk), getting rid of manual steps by automating processes, and having development and test environments that are as close as possible to the production environment.

The purpose of DevOps is to optimize the time from the development of an application until it's running stably in the production environment. The quicker you can get from idea to production, the quicker you can respond to changes in, and influences from, the market—which is crucial in order to have a successful business.

# Summary

This chapter has presented an overview of what ALM aims for and what it takes for the ALM platform to support a healthy ALM process. You've seen that ALM is the coordination and synchronization of all development lifecycle activities. There are four ways of looking at it:

- Software Development Lifecycle (SDLC) view

- Service management or operations view

- Application Portfolio Management (APM) view

- Unified view

Traceability, automation of high-level processes, and visibility into development processes are three pillars of ALM. Other key components are collaboration, work planning, workflow, security, reporting, analytics, being open-standards based, being plug-in friendly, and much more. A good ALM tool should help you implement and automate these pillars and components to deliver better business value to your company or organization.

# CHAPTER 2

■ ■ ■

# An Overview of TFS

This chapter discusses a tool that will make it clear why ALM is an important process for organizations engaged in IT development. A good implementation of ALM will help the organization deliver better business value to fulfill its business needs. Automating tasks by using tools such as Visual Studio 2015 and Team Foundation Server (TFS) 2015 can support this process.

In this chapter, you will learn how TFS can be used to fulfill the three main pillars of ALM and the issues addressed by ALM, which we covered in Chapter 1. We will start with an overview of ALM and of TFS and then move on to the specifics of using TFS for ALM.

## Application Lifecycle Management Overview

As you may recall from Chapter 1, there are three main pillars of an ALM process:

- *Traceability of relationships between artifacts:* The lack of traceability can be a major cost driver in any enterprise. There must be a way of tracing the requirements all the way to delivered code and back again—through architect models, design models, build scripts, unit tests, test cases, and so on. Practices such as test-driven development and configuration management can help, and these can be automated and supported by TFS.

- *Automation of high-level processes:* There are approval processes to control handoffs between analysis and design. There are other handoffs among build, deployment, testing, and so on. Much of this is done manually in many projects, and ALM stresses the importance of automating these tasks for a more effective and less time-consuming process.

- *Visibility into the progress of development efforts:* Many managers and stakeholders have limited visibility into the progress of development projects. Their visibility often comes from steering group meetings during which the project manager goes over the current situation. Other interest groups such as project members may also have limited visibility of the whole project even though they are part of it. This often occurs because reporting is hard to do and can involve a lot of manual work. Daily status reports can quite simply take too much time and effort to produce, for example, especially when we have information in many repositories.

© Joachim Rossberg 2016
J. Rossberg, *Agile Project Management using Team Foundation Server 2015*,
DOI 10.1007/978-1-4842-1870-9_2

Other important topics that ALM addresses are as follows:

- *Improving collaboration:* Collaboration is needed between teams, team members, stakeholders, and users, just to mention a few relationships. When development is spread around the world in different locations, collaboration can be hard to manage without the help of a proper tool.

- *Closing the gap between IT and business:* The big gap between IT and the business side of an organization is a serious problem for organizations, preventing companies from delivering the greatest business value they can achieve in their projects.

- *Using one tool:* The complexity of using several tools for solving project issues as a team member can be tough and costly as well. Switching between tools can be a cost driver. Using one tool to add plug-ins and use more features directly in an ordinary GUI instead of switching between applications is preferable. So, if you have several roles in a project, you can still use one tool to get the job done.

- *Enhancing role switching:* ALM also addresses the potential to use one tool when switching among different roles in a project. In many cases, project members play several roles in projects. A developer, for instance, might also work with tests or databases. If that person can use the same GUI for all tasks, there will be minimal overhead for switching between these roles.

# Team Foundation Server Overview

TFS has come a long way toward fulfilling the ALM vision, but it does not cover everything. TFS is an open and extensible product that will let you adjust its features to your needs and add the things it might lack at this point to support your specific needs. It is also important to know that Microsoft is spending a lot of time, energy, and money on developing this product further. It is not a toolset that will go away quickly (although one never knows); it is one of the most important toolsets in the Microsoft ecosystem.

TFS is now available in two versions; Team Foundation Server (TFS) and the cloud-based Visual Studio Team Services (VSTS). This book uses both versions for illustrations.

## Team Foundation Server

You can see that the heart of ALM in the Visual Studio 2015 world is TFS 2015 or if you use the cloud-based version, Visual Studio Team Services (formerly known as Visual Studio Online), as shown in Figure 2-1.

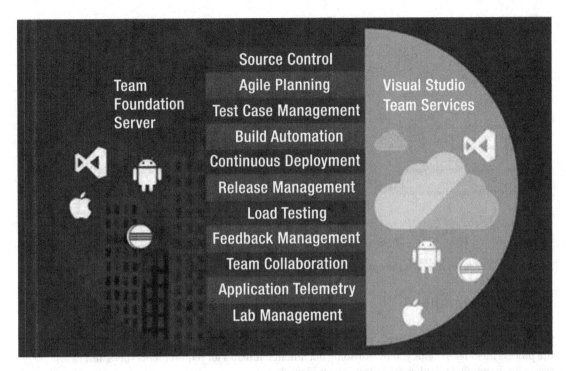

*Figure 2-1.* *An overview of Visual Studio 2015*

TFS exposes different functions and services for developers, project managers, and others like version control, reporting, and build and work item tracking. Not shown in the image is that TFS uses Microsoft SQL Server as its data repository.

---

■ **Note** Work items (Figure 2-2) are used to manage different types of information in TFS. We have work items for requirements, bugs, general tasks, and so on. To put it simply, a work item is a piece of work that must be completed in a project. The work item tracking system is one of the core parts of TFS for ALM process implementation.

---

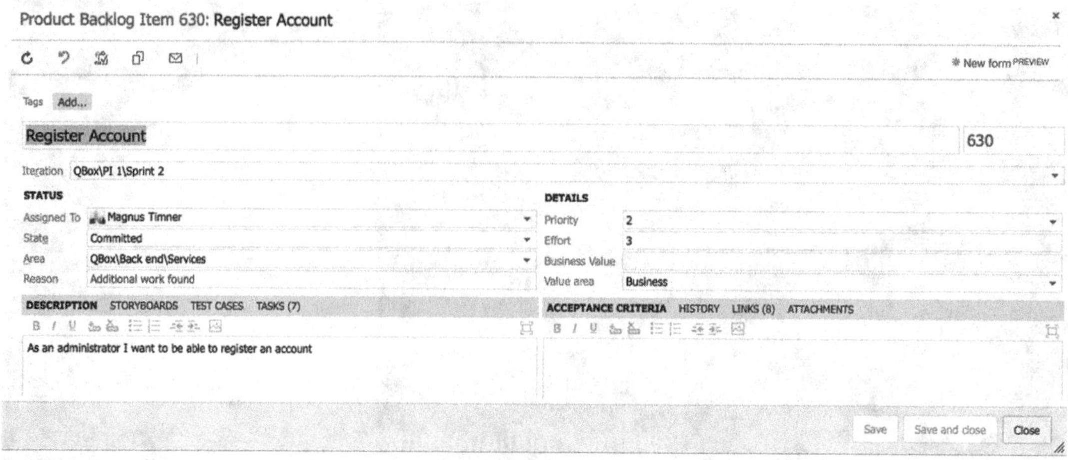

Product Backlog Item 630: Register Account
New form PREVIEW
Tags Add...
Register Account
630
Iteration QBox\PI 1\Sprint 2
STATUS
Assigned To Magnus Timner
State Committed
Area QBox\Back end\Services
Reason Additional work found
DETAILS
Priority 2
Effort 3
Business Value
Value area Business
DESCRIPTION STORYBOARDS TEST CASES TASKS (7)
As an administrator I want to be able to register an account
ACCEPTANCE CRITERIA HISTORY LINKS (8) ATTACHMENTS
Save
Save and close
Close

***Figure 2-2.*** *The heart of TFS is the work item—in this case, a product backlog work item*

# Process Template

What keeps all of these services together is the process template (see Figure 2-3) that sits on top of TFS/VSTS. This is a very interesting part of TFS. The template helps you visualize and automate tasks and steps that the process includes. It helps you by providing document templates for requirements specs, test cases, scenarios, handoffs, and other artifacts you should produce.

Process Templates
Team Foundation Server / Visual Studio Team Services

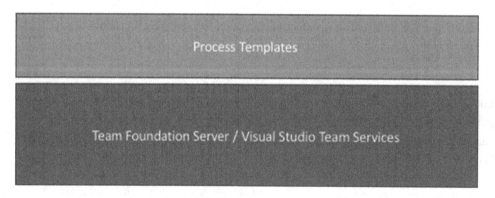

***Figure 2-3.*** *The process template customizes TFS behavior*

Most companies use some kind of process for their development or ALM. Even though some companies don't think they have a process, they do. The process might not be written down, but the company still has ways of doing things that in reality is the process—for instance, naming conventions, where to store builds, how to handle change requests, and so on.

In many cases, we have seen companies with lots of money invested in their processes. They have sent staff to training, provided large process manuals, and so on. However, they've had problems getting project members to actually use the processes in their daily work. The excuses are many: the process is hard to understand, remembering all the process steps is difficult, the process is not automated or included in the tools, and many others.

The end result has been that project members use their own variant of the process, causing confusion during the project's lifetime. This also causes severe problems, as handoffs between the development team and the operations team are often difficult. A typical bad scenario can occur when a system has to wait for deployment because the infrastructure isn't in place for the new system. Operations was not involved (or perhaps even informed) during the project and suddenly they are expected to run the system on hardware they don't have.

In TFS, you can implement your development process as a template that will be mandatory for all new projects. When you create a new project, you also create a new instance of the process template. You don't have to stop at the development project level either. You can implement most parts of the ALM cycle in the template as well, enabling you to take advantage of TFS all along the way. The template helps you visualize and automate tasks and steps that the process includes. It helps you by providing document templates for requirements specs, test cases, scenarios, handoffs, and other artifacts you should produce.

The template also provides information about which reports you have available for each new project— reports that you'll use to retrieve information about the status of projects and many other things. The template also contains information about one of the most important core parts of TFS: the work items. These can be adjusted as needed so you can make sure they contain the information the organization must have included with them. This information could be status information for a bug, for instance, such as Active, Resolved, or Closed.

This template is so flexible that you can develop and implement your own process, you can choose to use any of the three that Microsoft supplies, you can use a third-party template, or you can choose to customize the Microsoft templates to your own liking. You can also have several process templates in TFS so you can use different templates for different projects. Because TFS is not used to its full potential without the process templates, we cannot stress enough that you should consider which templates you want to use and the information you want them to include.

# Visual Studio 2015 Editions

Most developers will use Visual Studio to access the features of TFS. There are several editions available:

- *Visual Studio Community:* Full-featured Integrated Development Environment for building web, Windows desktop and cross-platform iOS, Android, and Windows apps. This edition is free for open source projects, academic research, training, education, and small professional teams.

- *Visual Studio Professional:* Professional developer tools and services for individual developers or small teams. Powerful features to improve your team's productivity such as CodeLens. Improve team collaboration with agile project planning tools, team rooms, charts, and more.

- *Visual Studio Enterprise:* Enterprise-grade solution with advanced capabilities for teams working on projects of any size or complexity, including advanced testing and DevOps. Build quality applications at scale with advanced features such as load testing, automated and manual testing, and IntelliTest capabilities. Manage complexity and resolve issues quickly with features such as Code Map and IntelliTrace.

- *Visual Studio Test Professional:* This is the tool for testers. These tools are also included in the Ultimate edition but it lacks the development tools included in the other editions.

- *Team Explorer Everywhere:* Enables developers on other platforms like Eclipse on the Mac to access TFS. This is the perfect add-on for teams with development on multiple platforms like .NET and Java.

# TFS Web

All projects in TFS have their own web sites available. By using Windows SharePoint Services or Server, a team project portal is created when the project itself is created. By using this portal, or the more advanced Team System Web Access, you can access most of the functionality in TFS. The project portal lets you access the parts of TFS that are available from inside Visual Studio, from an easy-to-use interface, especially for non-technical project members. Figure 2-4 shows what Web Access could look like.

**Figure 2-4.** *The Team System Web Access start page on TFS*

Many of our customers use a team project portal primarily to provide access to reports and work items for non-technical people not used to the Visual Studio interface. When we want to give an external user (such as a customer or remote stakeholder) access to work item creation and editing, or another more advanced task, we typically use Web Access.

# Microsoft Office

Microsoft Office can be used by project managers, product owners, or Scrum masters, for example, wishing to use tools that are familiar to them, such as Microsoft Project and Microsoft Office Excel, during a project. The integration is very nice and valuable to these roles.

# Integrated Development Environment (IDE) Integration

When it comes to add-ons, one thing we should mention in particular is the Team Explorer. This tool can be used as an add-on to Visual Studio, and it gives access to TFS directly from within Visual Studio. From here you can open reports, add new work items, and run queries against the TFS database.

TFS is a flexible tool, as we have mentioned. It is also very extensible, as all functionality can be accessed via web services. This is a very nice feature that enables you to build your own support for TFS in other applications, as well. Many third-party vendors have done this, and a wide array of add-ons and tools are available. Our favorite came from Teamprise, a company that has built add-ons to Eclipse so that we can use TFS features in our Java development environment as well. Teamprise was purchased by Microsoft, and its suite of client applications has been available as Team Explore Everywhere since TFS 2010. It offers the same IDE integration into both Eclipse and Visual Studio, allowing you to truly work as one team, no matter whether you use Eclipse or Visual Studio.

# Traceability

Having traceability in your ALM processes is key to the successful delivery and maintenance of applications and systems. I once visited a company that stopped making changes to its systems just because no one ever knew where a change (or bug fix) might have its impact. You don't have to live with such a situation.

These TFS features can help you with traceability so you can avoid such problems:

- Work item tracking
- Test-driven development/unit testing
- Automated builds/continuous delivery
- Check-in policies
- Version-control system

Let's look at some of the specifics involved with these features, starting with how the work item tracking system implements traceability.

## The TFS Work Item Tracking System

Sometimes it seems like we have tons of Post-its on our monitors and desks—each one containing at least one task we are supposed to take care of. We would like to track them in a tool that could help us, but often it just isn't possible. It could be that some tasks are connected with one project, others with another. We have tried writing them all down in an Excel spreadsheet and saving that to the computer. But soon we find that this spreadsheet is located on our laptops, our customer's computer, our desktops, another customer computer, and so on. And we have no idea which one is the current version.

The same thing often occurs in projects. Project managers have their to-do lists for a project, and they all have their own way of keeping them updated. Let's say a project manager (PM) uses Excel to keep track of these tasks—the status of tasks, to whom they are assigned, and so on. How can the PM keep the team updated with the latest to-do list? If the PM chooses to e-mail it, chances are that some people won't save the new version to disk or will just miss it in the endless stream of e-mail coming into their mailboxes. Soon there are various versions floating around, and things are generally a mess.

## Work Items

TFS has a task-tracking system at your service. We will take a closer look at work items in Chapter 4, so we will keep it brief here. The core of this system is represented by the tasks themselves, which as we said earlier are called *work items*. A work item can be pretty much what you want it to be. It can be a bug, a requirement of some sort, a general to-do item, and so on. Each work item has a unique ID that helps you keep track of the places it is referenced (see Figure 2-5). The work item ID (60 in Figure 2-5) lets you follow a work item, let's say a requirement, from its creation to its implementation as a piece of executable software (component).

Product Backlog Item 60: Create Expense Report

Create Expense Report|

Iteration | Expense Reporting\Release 1\Sprint 1

**STATUS**

| | | | **DETAILS** | |
|---|---|---|---|---|
| Assigned To | Harry Bryan | ▼ | Effort | 8 |
| State | New | ▼ | Business Value | |
| Reason | New backlog item | | Area | Expense Reporting ▼ |

**DESCRIPTION**  STORYBOARDS  TEST CASES  TASKS

B *I* U ≔ ≣ ≛ ≛ ⊠ ✗ ☒

As an Employee I want to have an efficient way to manage my expenses.

The following rules apply to an expense report:

1. It should be possible to create an expense report for project activities

2. It should be possible to create an expense report for internal activities

**ACCEPTANCE CRITERIA**  HISTORY  LINKS  ATTACHMENTS

B *I* U ≔ ≣ ≛ ≛ ⊠ ✗ ☒

1. An employee can create a project related expense report
2. An employee can create an internal expense report
3. An employee can update an expense report as long as it has not yet been approved.
4. All required fields must be provided to create an expense report
5. All optional fields may be provided to create an expense report

***Figure 2-5.*** *Each work item has a unique ID, in this case Product Backlog Item 60*

Work items provide a great way for you to simplify task management in a project while at the same time enabling traceability. No more is there confusion as to which version of the task list is the current one; no more manual labor for gathering status reports on work progress that are used only at steering group meetings. Now you have a solution that lets you collaborate more easily with your teams and enables all members and stakeholders to view status reports whenever they want. You can also more easily collaborate with people outside the project group by adding work items via the web client.

TFS is so flexible in this regard that it lets you tailor the work items as you want them to be. The work item tracking system is one of the core components of TFS. This system enables you to create work items, or units of work, and can be used to enable traceability. You can use the work items included with TFS from the beginning, or you can choose to adjust these to your needs, or even create your own work item types. Each work item instance has a unique ID that you can attach to the things you do in TFS. This enables you to follow one work item—let's say a requirement, for example—from its creation to its implementation as a piece of executable software (component). You can also associate one work item with others and build a hierarchy of work items.

The work items can contain information in different fields that define the data to be stored in the work item. This means that each field will have a name and a data type.

All work items can have different information attached to them. You can have information about to whom the work item is assigned and the status of the work at the moment (for example, a bug could be open, closed, under investigation, resolved, and so on). The State field can be modified so that each work item type can have its own state mechanism. This is logical because a bug probably goes through states different from those that a general task goes through, for instance. You can also attach documents to the work item and link one work item to other work items. You can even create a hierarchy of work items if you want. Let's say that you implement a requirement as a work item and that this requirement contains many smaller tasks. Then you can have the requirement itself at the top and nest the other requirements below that so you know which work items belong to which requirement.

When a bug is discovered, for instance, you can quickly follow the original requirement by its work item ID and see in which places in the code you might have to make some fixes. You can also see the associated work items so that you can evaluate whether other parts of the code need to be changed as a result of this bug fix.

TFS saves information about the work item on the data tier, which helps you follow the change history of the work item. You can see who created it, who resolved it, who closed it, and so on. The information in the databases can be used for display on reports, allowing you to tailor these depending on your needs. One report could show the status of all bugs, for instance. Stakeholders can see how many open bugs exist, how many are resolved, and much, much more. It is completely up to you and your organization how you choose to use the work items.

If you implement a requirement as a work item, you can use the work item ID to track this requirement through source code and to the final build of the executable system. By requiring all developers to add one or more work item IDs to the check-in using a check-in policy, you can enable this traceability.

## Configuration Management Using TFS

In any (development) organization, you need to have control of the versions of your systems you have in production. If you don't have that, the overall ALM process will suffer, because you will suddenly lose traceability. This will make it harder to implement changes and bug fixes, because you won't know which versions you need to update.

Without the help of a proper tool, you soon will get lost in the variety of applications you have. TFS can help you with this in many ways. After a brief description of software configuration management, I will cover three of the most important concepts that have great support in TFS and Visual Studio tools:

- Version control

- Release management

- Build management

---

■ **Note**   In software engineering, software configuration management (SCM) is the task of tracking and controlling changes in the software. Configuration management practices include revision control and the establishment of baselines and are very important. There are several goals of SCM, including the following:

*Configuration identification:* Ensuring that you know what code you are working with

*Configuration control:* Controlling the release of a product and its changes (version control)

*Build management:* Managing the process and tools used for builds

*Defect tracking:* Making sure every defect has traceability back to the source

If these issues are not covered by your ALM process, you could very soon find yourself in a troublesome situation. It is crucial for the development teams to have full control over which versions of the applications exist, which are in production, and where. This topic is closely related to the portfolio management team, and generally a big company has one or more persons devoted to keeping track of this.

---

### Version Control and Release Management in TFS 2015

Using the version-control system in TFS, you can manage and control multiple revisions of the same information in your projects. This information can be source code, documents, work items, and other important information that you want to add version control to. When you want to work on an item under source control, you check it out to your local computer so you can start working on it. When work is done and tested, you check in your changes so the version on the server is updated.

The version-control features of Team Foundation Server 2015 are powerful. They are fully integrated into the GUI, which is something that ALM prescribes as well. If you want to, you can access some of the features from a project portal as well. Many people want to use the command line for their work, and TFS enables them to use the command line for working with version control as well.

However, if you do want to use Visual Studio to access the TFS version-control system, you can do that. The extensibility of TFS makes this possible. One example of this is the Team Explorer Everywhere suite of client applications that can access TFS, including the version-control system. Teamprise has developed an Eclipse plug-in that lets users access TFS from Eclipse instead. Teamprise also lets you access TFS from Mac OS X and Linux command lines. This way, you can more easily integrate different development platforms in a TFS project. You still will use the TFS repository and have the ability to get reports and other information directly from TFS.

## Build Management

A *build* is basically the process of taking the source code and all other items necessary in an application and building it into executable software. Team Foundation Build is the build engine in TFS and executes the build process as defined by the TFS settings. Team Foundation Build is built on the Microsoft build engine (MSBuild), which is the build platform for Microsoft and Visual Studio. You can attach unit tests to a build process so that you automatically run these every time the build process kicks off. Team Foundation Build is fully integrated into the Visual Studio GUI so you don't have to use separate tools for handling these tasks.

Team Foundation Build supports several types of builds:

- *Full builds:* You build everything in the project. This can be resource- and time-consuming.

- *Partial builds:* You build only one or more parts of the system.

- *Nightly builds:* Many projects build the system during nighttime. Especially if the build process takes a long time, this can be very handy.

- *Custom builds:* You can use the extensibility of TFS to create your own build types or edit any of the existing ones.

- *Incremental builds:* You build only the components that have been changed since the last build.

You can also add a number of tasks that you want to be executed when running the build:

- Get the latest source code from the version-control system

- Compile sources

- Perform architectural validation

- Run static analysis tool

- Execute unit tests

- Update work items

- Perform code coverage

- Calculate code churn (how many rows of code have been modified or added since the last count)

- Produce build reports

- Drop exe/output into predefined location

# Automation of High-Level Processes

Without one or more templates, TFS will not be used to its full potential, as you saw earlier in this chapter. You could still use its version-control system and some other tools, but the real value comes from using it to automate your ALM process. In the process template, your whole ALM process is defined. Chapters 5 and 6 cover a lot more on this topic as well.

The template defines the following:

- *Work item types*: Which work item types are necessary and what information they should have attached to them. You can also define the workflow for a work item. For a bug, you might have different states the item flows through, such as Active, Resolved, Closed, and so on.

- *Project phases*: By using areas and iterations, you can define the initial project phase setup of your projects. If you use RUP (https://en.wikipedia.org/wiki/Rational_Unified_Process), you can define the process phases in that model, or you can create the first sprints of a Scrum project. Areas and iterations are flexible, and you can create your own way of working through these concepts.

- *Document structure and templates*: The number of documents that should be produced during a project will differ depending on your process model. In the process template, you define the document structure you need and the templates you should use. For instance, you can add templates for requirement specifications or acceptance testing here.

- *Reports and queries*: In the process template, you can specify which reports and work item queries you need to have as defaults in your projects. You probably want reports and queries showing the progress of your project, such as the status of bugs or work remaining. You can create your own reports by using SQL Server Reporting Services or Excel and add them to all projects by adjusting the process template.

- *Security*: The template also adds information about which users or user groups have access to what information. You can connect TFS groups to your Active Directory accounts, for instance.

The process template is the overall process for your ALM implementation. Many of our customers create different templates for different kinds of projects. They also create templates for operations, so that when a development project is finished and deployed, the operations staff can use their template to run the system until the system dies. A few customers have started creating a template for Information Technology Infrastructure Library (ITIL), for instance, and we are looking forward to seeing the result of that work.

It is important to remember that you can adjust the process to your needs. You should consider changing the default templates or even replacing them, rather than adjusting your own way of working to the templates that come with TFS out of the box. Microsoft enables this flexibility by letting you easily access the process templates to adjust them or to add new templates.

# Visibility

Information about project status is important to all participants of a project—and we don't mean team members only, but stakeholders and decision makers as well. As project managers, we have spent too much time chasing down information to answer questions about the status of projects, how much work remains, and what the latest bug status is.

TFS provides two primary ways of enabling visibility:

- *Reports*: Reports are created by using SQL Server Reporting Services (for more information, check out *Pro SQL Server 2012 Reporting Services, 3rd Edition,* by Apress) and accessing the TFS data tier directly. You can define and adjust these as you want. You can also use Excel to create reports if you prefer.

- *Queries*: Queries are used to ask questions of the work item tracking service. One question might be how many bug work items you have. How many and which are dedicated to me? How many bugs are there? And so on. You can create new queries when necessary.

By using these two components, it will be easier to gather the information you need for your status reports for a steering group meeting or project meeting. You won't have to look around in several places and in several applications for this information anymore; instead, you can use the automated reports and queries from inside TFS.

Project owners, project managers, and Scrum masters will certainly benefit from TFS. Because TFS has all data in the same repository, you can more easily retrieve the correct information when you want it. The flexibility of the SQL Server database that stores all information is great. You can work with the data warehouse information just as you would with any other database.

By using the project portal or TFS Web (see Figure 2-6), you can publish information (in the form of custom-built controls that users cannot change at this time) so that everybody who has privileges can see them. This is an easy way to make sure that information is available all the time. Just this little, relatively non-technical improvement will off-load work from the project manager, freeing some of the PM's or PO's time for better things.

**Figure 2-6.** *Viewing reports from TFS Web*

# Collaboration

As you know, TFS comes with Team Explorer, which is an add-on to Visual Studio. With this tool, the developer can access every aspect of a TFS project. The developer can view reports and queries, for instance, as well as access the document in the project. The developer can access the version control system as well as build systems, tests, and so on.

The Team Explorer is full featured but is still a tool for people used to working in Visual Studio. For us that is no problem, but for most project managers and stakeholders, the GUI is confusing. They want to have an easier-to-use tool to access the relevant information.

Each project that is created with TFS has a project portal created as well. This portal provides access to reports, documents, project process guidance, and other project-related information through a web interface. This enables people who are not used to the Visual Studio interface to easily retrieve the information they need.

There is also a collaboration site called *team room* (see Figure 2-7) that is created for each TFS Team Project. This is a collaboration area where team members can chat, share information, and let TFS display information about different status aspects (such as how the nightly build went).

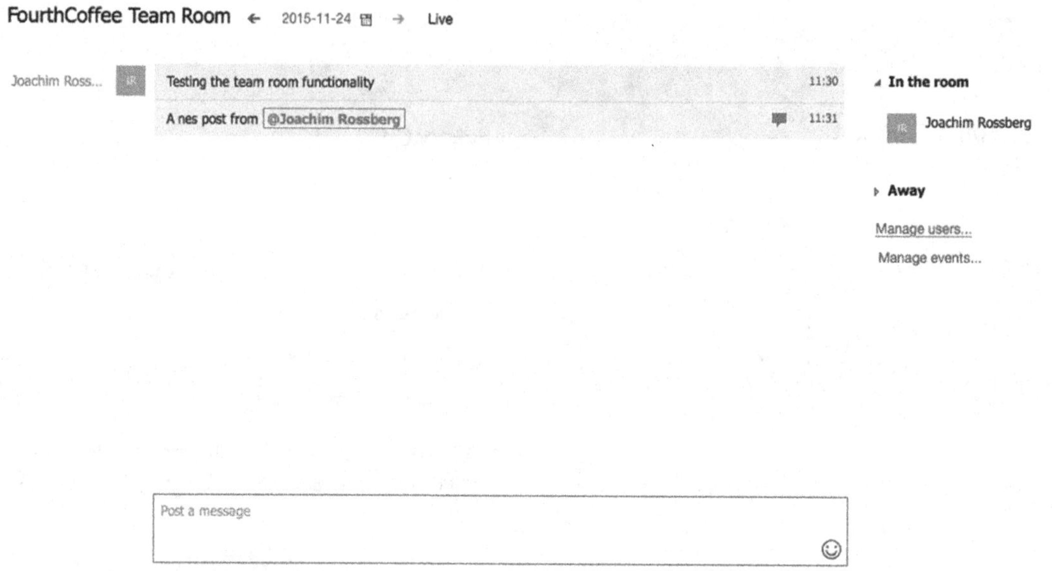

*Figure 2-7.* *The TFS team room*

Collaboration, of course, does not only mean giving access to information, even though this is as important as any other means of collaboration. Collaboration also means that you should be able to work together to fulfill one or more goals.

## Work Items for Collaboration

You can use the work item features of TFS to enable your process workflows. Let's say a project manager, or anybody responsible for inputting requirements as work items into TFS, creates a new work item of the Scenario type. This scenario should probably be assigned to a developer to implement. The project manager uses the work item system to assign (see Figure 2-8) the scenario to a specific developer, in this case Joachim. Joachim continues to work on the scenario until it is ready for testing. He then assigns the work item to a tester who performs the testing. When the testing is done, the work item is perhaps closed. If a bug is found, either the tester or anyone finding the bug can use the work item tracking system to see who developed the scenario implementation and reassign it to that developer, in this case, Joachim again. TFS keeps track of who has worked on the work item so that you don't have to manually keep track of this.

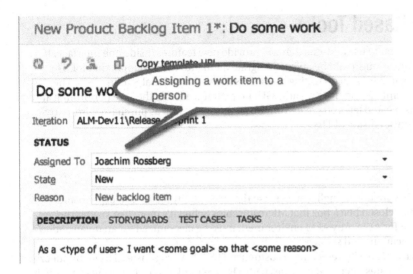

*Figure 2-8. Assigning work items to a specific person*

# The Gap Between IT and Business

Closing the gap between IT and business is obviously a very tough problem to solve. TFS won't get you all the way, that's for sure. We don't think any tool ever will because so much depends on the people in the organizations, which is an important consideration. But tools can help you bridge the gap, so you should carefully consider how you can use them for this. We need to improve on our ALM process and way of working to start solving this. When we have a new way of working, TFS can support much of our efforts using, for instance, the process template to implement this new way of working.

The gap between the IT and business sides is often a question of work process. It requires considering many things, and when you have a solution or start working toward a solution, you must evaluate which parts of this work process you can automate and use tools for solving. One thing worth mentioning here is that the use of the TFS Project Server Connector with TFS lets you integrate TFS with Microsoft Office Project Server. Having this integration will allow you to better control your resources and better automate this process as well. This way, you can align your portfolio management process better so that you can choose which things to work on more effectively.

# Office/MS Project Integration

When we have run projects in the past, we mostly used Microsoft Office Project to handle project planning, especially the Gantt diagram. We suspect that this is the case for many of our fellow project managers as well. In many cases, we have used this product not primarily because of the tool itself but because so many of our customers use Microsoft Office that it becomes natural for them to also use Project. Project has its strengths and weaknesses, as all tools do, and we cannot say that we don't like it, but we have never become friends with it. Sometimes it does things that we don't expect, and even though we know this is because we are not very familiar with its features, we still blame the product from time to time—unfair, but that's life sometimes.

Excel and Project are two tools that most companies use on both the business and the IT sides of the company. By being able to use these tools, business people can more easily be a part of the ALM process, because they can use a tool they are already used to working with. A nice feature here is that the communication between Office and TFS is two-way. This means that an update in TFS will be reflected in Office and the other way around. This allows for a dynamic way of working with TFS information.

# Use of One Role-Based Tool

A good ALM tool should enable you to use add-ons that will provide new features inside one interface. If a developer needs testing features, you should be able to integrate them into the development tool. The developer should not have to switch tools to do testing tasks. This is also what Visual Studio offers. There is no context switching as team members can use the same GUI no matter what role they are performing at the moment. TFS is also extensible and lets you create your own add-ons as well as purchase third-party add-ons that will be accessible from inside of TFS.

# Extensibility

When the built-in features of TFS are not enough, you can use the extensibility features to expand and enhance it. TFS is often seen as a closed black box that Microsoft ships, when it's more like an enterprise resource planning (ERP) system for ALM. Any ALM environment must be customized for an organization's processes and the existing applications and services.

Many of our customers have been a bit reluctant to customize TFS. They have instead tried to squeeze their way of working into the templates Microsoft provides with TFS. We think this is the wrong way to do it. Our suggestion is that you start the other way around. Start by asking yourself how your organization wants to work. This process involves all parts of the organization, from the business side to operations. Try to find agreement on how to work in the ALM process. By doing so, you will see that this also is a good start for collaboration in the company.

For instance, consider the work items and the information in them. If the fields and information in the MSF templates are not enough, extend or edit them. TFS lets you do this by changing the process template. You can choose to add the information that you need, and it will be stored in the TFS databases, so you can have access to it from within your reports and queries. Don't forget to change the reports or queries, as well; otherwise, you will not see your information.

Some of our customers have changed the workflow of a work item by adding more states to it, when the ones supplied have not been enough. Often we have used the TFS Power Tools to do this.

When you have an initial idea of how you want to conduct the ALM process, start looking into what TFS gives you out of the box. Use what can be used, change other things, and build your own solution where needed.

One great strength of TFS is its extensibility and flexibility. You can adjust the whole tool to fit most parts of your ALM process. If you want to, you can develop your own add-ons by giving support to roles not included from the start. We strongly encourage you to use these extensibility features, but in the end it is your choice.

Extensibility is a great way to integrate existing systems and potentially migrate some of them into TFS in order to reduce the toolset in the organization.

# Differences Between TFS and VSTS

VSTS is cloud-based. This is also the version of Team Foundation Server where Microsoft deploys all new features first. Every three weeks Microsoft aims to update VSTS. These updates are then packaged to a TFS update that is released approximately every three months. Table 2-1 shows an overview of the difference in features between TFS and VSTS.

Keep in mind that the information in Table 2-1 will change as time goes by. VSTS is updated every three weeks with new functionality and the differences between the two will probably diminish.

*Table 2-1.* *A Comparison Between TFS and VSTS*

|  | TFS | VSTS |
|---|---|---|
| Work items, version control, and build | ✓ | ✓ |
| Agile product/project management | ✓ | ✓ |
| Test case management | ✓ | ✓ |
| Heterogeneous development (Eclipse, Git) | ✓ | ✓ |
| Ease of installation and setup | Good | Better |
| Collaborate with anyone, from anywhere | Good | Better |
| Data stays inside your network | ✓ | ✗ |
| Process template and work item customization | ✓ | ✗ |
| SharePoint integration | ✓ | ✗ |
| Data warehouse and reporting | ✓ | ✗ |
| CodeLens support | ✓ | ✓ |
| Cloud load testing | ✗ | ✓ |
| Application insights | ✗ | ✓ |
| Always running the latest version of TFS | ✗ | ✓ |

# Summary

In our opinion, Team Foundation Server can help you implement a good, automated, and robust ALM process. There are features for all aspects of ALM. Correctly used, these features will help you improve your ALM process, which in the end will give you better business value and more successful projects.

The three pillars of ALM—traceability, process automation, and visibility—are all important for any organization to have. TFS is a great foundation on which to build ALM solutions. TFS has work item tracking for traceability, process template implementation in the tool itself for process automation, and reports and queries for visibility. Through a project portal, accessible via the Internet, you can improve collaboration among all parties having an interest in your projects.

TFS is role based in the sense that it supports different development roles. It has support for architects, developers, DBAs, testers, and more. They are not separate tools either, but they are all accessible from a unified GUI. You can also add custom add-ons to the GUI and do not have to use several tools to get the job done.

Product owners and project managers have the capability to use tools they are already familiar with. Most use Excel or Project for project planning, and there is integration between these tools and TFS. You can easily sync information among these tools.

The extensibility of TFS makes it fairly easy to write your own code integrating TFS with other applications. This is an incredible strength of TFS, and something we should give Microsoft credit for.

So, all in all, Team Foundation Server is a great foundation on which to build your Application Lifecycle Management process.

■ ■ ■

# CHAPTER 3

# Introduction to Scrum and Agile Concepts

Our experience is that there has been a great deal of improvement in projects over the last decade. To be more specific, we've seen the agile movement make an impact on how projects deliver business value.

The focus of this book, when it comes to processes and frameworks, is on agile methods like Scrum and XP. The reason is simply that agile fits nicely with the concept of ALM.

This chapter looks at how you can use Scrum as an agile project-management model to deliver software. We cover the Scrum process in-depth, including how you in practice can use Scrum and agile practices such as agile estimation and planning in combination with an ALM tool. This chapter gives you insight into why agile and ALM are a good match.

This chapter also shows you some other agile processes that are popular. Scrum in itself is a great framework, but some projects and organizations need another process to help run their projects.

## The Scrum Framework

Next is one of our favorite development models: Scrum. With all the attention Scrum has been getting in recent years, you may be misled into believing it's a fairly new model. The truth is that the Scrum approach, although not called Scrum at the time, was first presented as "the rugby approach" in 1986. In the January-February 1986 issue of the *Harvard Business Review*, Hirotaka Takeuchi and Ikujiro Nonaka described this approach for the first time.[1] In the article, they argued that small cross-functional teams produced the best results from a historical viewpoint.

It wasn't until 1990, however, that the rugby approach was referred to as *Scrum*. In 1990, Peter DeGrace and Leslie Hulet Stahl[2] highlighted this term from Takeuchi's and Nonaka's original article. The term comes from rugby originally (see Figure 3-1), where it means the quick, safe, and fair restart of a rugby game after a minor infringement or stoppage.[3] This is also the source of the following quotation:

---

[1]Hirotaka Takeuchi and Ikujiro Nonaka, "The New New Product Development Game," *Harvard Business Review*, Jan/Feb 1986, https://hbr.org/1986/01/the-new-new-product-development-game.
[2]Peter DeGrace and Leslie Hulet Stahl, "Wicked Problems, Righteous Solutions," 1990, http://www.gbv.de/dms/ilmenau/toc/608728446.PDF.
[3]www.planetrugby.com.

© Joachim Rossberg 2016
J. Rossberg, *Agile Project Management using Team Foundation Server 2015*,
DOI 10.1007/978-1-4842-1870-9_3

**Figure 3-1.** *A real scrum!*

A scrum is formed in the field when eight players from each team, bound together in three rows for each team, close up with their opponents so that the heads of the front rows are interlocked. This creates a tunnel into which a scrum-halt throws in the ball so that front-row players can compete for possession by hooking the ball with either of their feet"

Keep this definition in mind as we describe the development version of Scrum.

Ken Schwaber started using Scrum at his company in the early 1990s. But to be fair, Jeff Sutherland was the first to call it Scrum.[4] Schwaber and Sutherland teamed up and presented this approach publicly in 1996 at Object-Oriented Programming, Systems, Languages, and Applications (OOPSLA) in Austin, Texas. They collaborated to use their experience and industry best practices to refine the model until it achieved its present look. Schwaber described the model in *Agile Software Development with Scrum* in 2001.[5]

Let's continue bay looking at empirical process control and see what that means in software development.

## Empirical Process Control

What is this model, or framework, all about? First, let's define two ways to solve problems. We touched on the issues with projects in Chapter 1. When you have an issue that is similar time after time (like road construction, for example, or implementing a standard system), you pretty much know what to expect from the various tasks at hand. You can then easily use a process—the Waterfall model, perhaps—that produces acceptable-quality output over and over again.[6] This approach is called *defined process control*.

---

[4]Jeff Sutherland, "Agile Development: Lessons Learned from the First Scrum," 2004, www.scrumalliance.org/resources/35.
[5]Ken Schwaber and Mike Beedle, *Agile Software Development with Scrum* (Prentice Hall, 2001).
[6]Ken Schwaber, *The Enterprise and Scrum* (Microsoft Press, 2007).

When it comes to a more complex problem, however, like building a software system, you saw earlier that the traditional models don't work. You then must use something called *empirical process control*, according to Schwaber.[7] Empirical process control has three legs to stand on:

- Transparency
- Inspection
- Adaptation

"Transparency means that the aspects of the process that affect the outcome must be visible to those controlling the process."[8] This means to be able to approve the outcome, you must agree on the criteria for the outcome. Two people can't say they're "done" with a task unless they both agree on what the criteria for "done" are.

The next leg is inspection. The process must be inspected as frequently as necessary to find unacceptable variances in it. Because any inspection may lead to a need to make changes to the process itself, you also need to revise the inspections to fit the new process. To accomplish this, you need skilled inspectors who know what they're inspecting.

The last leg is adaptation. An inspection may lead to a change in the process: this is one example of an adaptation. Another is that you must adapt the material being processed as a result of an inspection. All adaptations must be made as quickly as possible to minimize deviation later.

Schwaber reuses the example of code review when he discusses empirical process control. "The code is reviewed against coding standards and industry best practices. Everyone involved in the review fully and mutually understands these standards and best practices. The code review occurs whenever someone feels that a section of code is complete. The most experienced developers review the code, and their comments and suggestions lead to the developer adjusting his or her code."[9] Simple, isn't it? We could not have said it better ourselves.

## Complexity in Projects

What makes a software development process so complex? We discussed this a little previously, but let's dive deeper here. In theory, building a software system may seem pretty straightforward. You write code that logically instructs the CPU to control the computer. How hard can it be? Alas, it isn't that simple, we're afraid. The people writing the code are complex machines in themselves. They have different backgrounds, IQs, EQs, views, attitudes, and so on. Their personal lives also add to their complexity.

The requirements may also be complex and have a tendency to change over time. According to Schwaber, a large percentage of the requirements gathered at the beginning of a software project change during the project. And 60% of the features you build are rarely or never used in the end. Many times in our projects, several people at the customer site are responsible for the requirements. Often they have diverging agendas as to why and what to build. Often the stakeholders have a hard time expressing what they really want. Only when they see a first prototype of the system do they fully begin to see the possibilities of the software, and only then can they begin to understand what they want.

Rarely is it the case that just one computer is involved in a system, either. Generally there is interaction among several machines. You may have a web farm for your GUI, a cluster for your application tier, a backend SQL server, some external web services, and often a legacy system, all needing to integrate to solve the needs of the new system.

---

[7]Ibid.
[8]Ibid.
[9]Ibid.

When complex things interact—as people, requirements, and technology do in a software project—the level of complexity increases greatly. So it's safe to say that we don't have any simple software problems anymore. They're all complex. Schwaber realizes this as well. Figure 3-2 shows his complexity-assessment graph.

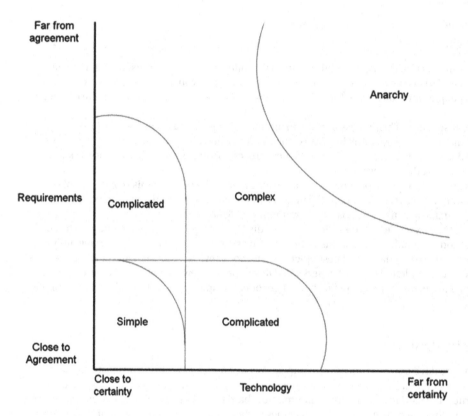

**Figure 3-2.** *Schwaber's complexity graph*

The projects in the anarchy area are chaotic and unworkable. To get them to their finish lines, you probably need to resolve serious issues before starting them.

What Scrum tries to do is address this inherent complexity by implementing inspection, adaptation, and visibility, as you previously saw in the section "Empirical Process Control." Scrum does so by having simple practices and rules.

## What Scrum Is

Scrum is a powerful, iterative, and incremental process. Many are fooled by its perceived simplicity, but it takes time to master. Figure 3-3 shows the skeleton of the Scrum model, to which we attach the rules and practices. In Scrum, you do development in time-boxed intervals called *iterations*. An iteration is usually between two and four weeks. Each iteration consists of daily inspections. Such an inspection—or daily Scrum, as it's called—is performed by the team once every day at a preset time.

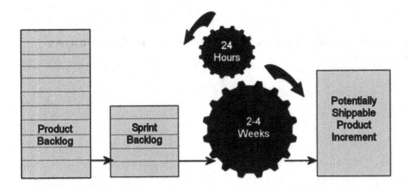

*Figure 3-3.* *The Scrum skeleton*

During these inspections, team members evaluate each other's work and the activities performed since the last inspection. If necessary adjustments (*adaptations*) are found, they're implemented as quickly as possible. The iterations also conclude with inspections, when more adaptations can be made. This cycle repeats until it's no longer funded.

All the requirements that are known at the beginning of the project are gathered in the product backlog, which is one of the artifacts of Scrum. We come back to this shortly. The project team reviews the backlog and selects which requirements should be included in the first iteration, or *sprint,* as it's called in Scrum. These selected requirements are added to the sprint backlog, where they're broken down into more detailed items (*tasks*). Later in the chapter, in Figure 3-9, you can see how many teams visualize their work in a sprint using a Scrum board. This can be electronic, as in the figure, or it can be a whiteboard with sticky notes. The board shows the tasks that have been found for each backlog item and where in the development process each task is currently located (development, test, and so on).

The team then makes its best effort to turn the sprint backlog into a shippable increment of the final product. The team is self-managing, which means members collectively decide who does what and what the best way is to solve problems.

The increment is presented to the stakeholder(s) at the end of the sprint so they can inspect it and make any adaptations necessary to the project. The sprint is most often 30 days, although as mentioned earlier, we often see sprints that last two to four weeks. It depends on the sprint backlog items. When I took his Scrum master certification, Ken Schwaber related that he once had a one-week sprint in a project. The reason was that the team malfunctioned, and this way he could more easily catch the reason and adjust the process so the project ran more smoothly.

The stakeholders' adaptations and feedback are put into the product backlog and prioritized again. Then the team starts the process over and selects the backlog items they think they can finish during the next sprint. These are put into the sprint backlog for the next sprint and broken down into more manageable items. And so it continues, until the stakeholders think they have received the business value they want and funding stops.

If you look again at the three legs of empirical process control, you can see that Scrum covers them nicely. Transparency is implemented by letting the team and stakeholders agree on the expected outcome of the project and of each iteration. Inspection occurs daily and also at the end of each sprint. Adaptations are the direct result of these inspections and a necessary thing in Scrum.

# Roles in Scrum

Scrum incorporates different roles. In other models, there are usually many more roles defined in a very strict way, but Scrum has only these three roles:

- The product owner

- The team

- The Scrum master

## The Product Owner

Let's start with the *product owner*. This person is responsible to those funding the project to deliver a product or a system that gives the best return on investment (ROI) he or she can get from the project. The product owner must acquire the initial funding for the project and make sure it's funded through its lifespan. The product owner represents everyone with a stake in the project and its result. At the beginning of a project, the product owner gathers the initial requirements and puts them into the product backlog. It's the product owner who ultimately decides which requirements have the highest priority based on ROI or business value (for example) and decides into which sprint they should go. During the project, the product owner inspects the project and prioritizes the product backlog and sprint backlogs so that the stakeholders' needs are met.

## The Team

The *team* is responsible for development. There are no specific roles on the team. Because the team is cross-functional and self-organizing, it's the members' responsibility to make sure they have the competencies and staff required for solving the problems. It isn't the Scrum master who decides who does what and when, as a project manager would do in a traditional approach. These are some of the reasons behind this approach, as taught by Ken Schwaber in his Scrum master course:

- People are most productive when they manage themselves.

- People take their commitment more seriously than other people's commitment for them (like when a project manager commits that a person should accomplish something).

- People always do the best they can.

- Under pressure to work harder, developers automatically and increasingly reduce quality.

The team should consist of seven people plus or minus two for optimal results. An optimal *physical team* consists of 2.5 *logical teams*. A logical team consists of one programmer, one tester, a half-time analyst/designer, and a half-time technical writer. The team decides which items in the backlog it can manage for each sprint based on the prioritized backlog.

This thinking is a giant leap from traditional project management and takes some getting used to. Some people don't accept it and find it impossible to work this way.

## The Scrum Master

The *Scrum master* is responsible for the Scrum process and has to make sure everybody on the team, the product owner, and anyone else involved in the project know and understand the process. The Scrum master makes sure everyone follows the rules and practices of the Scrum process. But the Scrum master doesn't manage the team—the team is, as you saw, self-managing.

If a conflict occurs in the team, the Scrum master should be the "oil" that helps the team work out its problems smoothly. It's also the Scrum master's responsibility to protect the team from the outside world so members can work in peace and quiet during the sprint, focused on delivering business value. The following are the Scrum master's responsibilities, again according to Ken Schwaber's course material:

- Removing the barriers between development and the customer so the customer directly drives development

- Teaching the stakeholders how to maximize ROI and meet their objectives through Scrum

- Improving the lives of the development team by facilitating creativity and empowerment

- Improving the productivity of the development team in any way possible

- Improving the engineering practices and tools so each increment of functionality is potentially shippable

## The Scrum Process

Now that you know the basics of Scrum, it's time to take a look at what happens during a Scrum project. The product owner, after arranging initial funding for the project, puts together the product backlog by gathering functional as well as non-functional requirements. The focus is on turning the product backlog into functionality, and it's prioritized so the requirements giving the greatest business value or having the highest risk come first. Remember that this approach is a value-up paradigm where you set business value first.

---

■ **Note**   *Value up* measures value delivered at each point in time and treats the inputs as variable flows rather than as a fixed stock. If you want to learn more about this, see *Software Engineering with Microsoft Visual Studio Team System* by Sam Guckenheimer (Addison Wesley, 2006).

---

Then the product backlog is divided into suggested releases (if necessary), which should be possible to implement immediately. This means when a release is finished, you should be able to put it into production at once so you can start getting the business value as quickly as possible. You don't have to wait until the entire project is done to begin getting return on your stakeholders' investments.

Because the Scrum process is adaptive, this is just the starting point. The product backlog and the priorities change during the project as business requirements change and also depending on how well the team succeeds in producing functionality. The constant inspections also affect the process.

When a sprint is starting, it initiates with a *sprint planning meeting*. At this meeting, the product owner and the team decide, based on the product owner's prioritization, what will be done during this sprint. The items selected from the product backlog are put into the sprint backlog.

The sprint planning meeting is time-boxed and can't last more than eight hours. The reason for this strict time-box is that the team wants to avoid too much paperwork about what should be done.

The meeting has two parts. The first four hours include the team and the product owner: the latter presents the highest-priority product backlog issues, and the team questions the product owner about those issues so members know what the requirements mean. The next four hours are used by the team to plan the sprint and break down the selected product backlog items (PBIs) into the sprint backlog.

When the project is rolling, each day starts with a 15-minute daily Scrum or stand-up meeting (see Figure 3-4). This is the 24-hour inspection. During this meeting, each team member answers three questions:

- What did I do yesterday that helped the development team meet the sprint goal?

- What will I do today to help the development team meet the sprint goal?

- Do I see any impediment that prevents me or the development team from meeting the sprint goal?

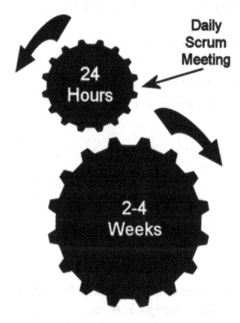

**Figure 3-4.** *The sprint in Scrum*

The reason for this meeting is to catch problems and hence be able to make timely adjustments to the process. It's the Scrum master's responsibility to help team members get rid of any impediments they may have.

When a sprint comes to an end, the stakeholders perform a *sprint review*. This meeting is also time-boxed, but at four hours instead of eight. The product owner and the stakeholders get a chance to see what the team has produced during the sprint and reflect on it. But it's important to remember that this meeting isn't a demonstration: it's a collaborative meeting of the people involved.

Now there is only one meeting left: the *sprint retrospective*. It takes place between the sprint review and the next sprint planning meeting. It's time-boxed at three hours. The Scrum master encourages the team to adjust the development process, still within the Scrum process and practices framework boundaries, so that the process can be more effective for the next sprint.

Some think that documentation and planning aren't necessary in Scrum. Developers like this idea because they don't want to write documents, whereas stakeholders tremble at the thought. But nothing could be further from the truth. Scrum doesn't say you don't document or a plan. The contrary is true. Planning, for instance, is done every day, during the daily Scrum (see Figure 3-5). Documents should also be written, but you scale away documents that aren't necessary—those that are produced only for the sake of documentation and are almost never read after they're produced. You document what is needed for the system and the project. You document your code, you document traceability, and so on.

**Traditional Project**

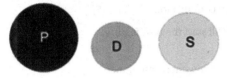

**Scrum Project**

**P = Planning**
**D = Development**
**S = Stabilization**

*Figure 3-5. Planning in Scrum*

That's basically it. Scrum is a lean process and appeals a great deal to us. Joachim had the privilege of doing his Scrum master certification during a course held by Ken Schwaber and his product owner certification training at a course held by Mike Cohn; these are two of the legends in the agile world. Unfortunately, some customers and stakeholders find Scrum a bit vague, so they won't try it. They think they have more control with the way they used to run projects and are perhaps afraid to embrace this modern way of doing projects. This hasn't changed over the years, although more and more people we meet have seen what Scrum and agile can do to help them run better projects.

We've found that some companies think they're using Scrum just because they develop iteratively. In many cases, they have changed the Scrum process so that it won't help them solve their development problems—problems that are clearly visible in a true Scrum project. Instead, they use Scrum like makeup to cover the bad spots; and when the project still fails, they argue that Scrum doesn't work—they still don't deliver value, they still have overruns, and so on. When you're implementing Scrum, follow the process and framework, and adjust the organization to Scrum, not the Scrum process to the organization. This can be a real problem in some organizations where, as we said, management resists change and won't use Scrum or agile for the simple reason that they think they will lose control. If you aren't in a position to enforce a new way of working, you need to consider how to most efficiently push management in the agile direction.

# Definition of Done

The Definition of Done (DoD) is very important, but it also tends to be forgotten. In many projects, at the end of (or during) a sprint or the project, we've seen arguments between the delivering development organization and the person ordering the project about whether a task has been done. Perhaps testing was not done the way the client assumed it would be, or the software doesn't comply with certain regulations. The following conversation is typical:

> The product owner (PO), Sofia, stops by the office of developer Mike to check on how things are going.
>
> S: "Hi. How's the new cool feature you're working on coming along?"
>
> M: "It's going great. I'm done with it right now and will start the next feature soon."
>
> S: "Great! Then I can show it to our customer, who's coming here after lunch. He'll be very excited!"
>
> M: "No, no. Hold on. I am not 'done' done with it. I still need to fix some test cases, do some refactoring, get it into the build process, and so on. I thought you were wondering if I had gotten somewhere with it ..."

For the most part, such arguments can be avoided if people sit down together at the beginning and write and sign a DoD.

There are other reasons for having a DoD, as well. In order for the team to estimate a user story, the members need to know when they're done with it. Otherwise, it's very hard to complete the estimate. For a specific user story, you know it's done when you've fulfilled its acceptance criteria. But where do all those general things like style guides, code analysis, build automation, test automation, regulatory compliance, governance, non-functional requirements, and so on, fit in? They affect the estimate of a user story as well.

Here is where the DoD comes into play. The DoD tells you what requirements in addition to the user story's acceptance criteria you need to fulfill in order to be done with the story. You include the general requirements in the DoD because they affect all user stories in the end.

The DoD is your primary quality document. If you don't fulfill what is in it, you don't deliver quality. It's essential that the PO and the team agree on the DoD. The DoD is part of the agreement between the team and the PO.

There shouldn't be an argument over this concept during the project. If the PO thinks it's too costly to use pair programming or test-driven development (TDD), have the PO sign the DoD, which specifies that these things have been removed. If, at the end of a sprint, the PO complains about the number of bugs, you can present the document and say that the PO removed essential parts of the testing process, and hence bugs will be present.

A good starting point for a DoD for an approved user story could be something like the following:

- All code is written and checked in (including tests)
- Coding conventions have been fulfilled (these are documented in a separate document and not included here)
- All unit tests have been passed (must be okay before check-in)
- Code is refactored (improved/optimized without change of function)
- All code has been reviewed by at least two people (peer programming or peer review)
- The user story is included in the build (build scripts updated, all new modules included)

- The user story is installable (build scripts updated so the story is included in the automatic install)
- All acceptance tests have been passed:
    - Acceptance criteria must exist
    - Acceptance tests are implemented (automatic or manual tests)
- The backlog has been updated as follows:
    - All tasks' remaining time is 0
    - The user story state is Done
    - Actual Hours has been updated
    - All tasks are Done
- The user story has been installed on Demoserver
- The user story has been reviewed by the PO
- The user story has been approved by the PO
- Product documentation has been updated and checked in
- A user manual has been written
- The administrative manual has been updated
- Help texts have been written

You could also have a DoD like the following for when the sprint is finished:

- All user stories in the sprint fulfill the DoD
- The product has been versioned (release management/rollback)
- All accepted bugs have been corrected
- New bugs that have been identified are closed and/or parked
- 80% code coverage from automated tests is fulfilled
- All chores are done and approved
- All integration tests have been passed
- The sprint retrospective has taken place, and actions for improvements have been identified
- The sprint review has taken place with the PO present
- A performance test of the complete system has been done

Let's continue by looking at how you can manage requirements and estimations with an agile mindset.

## Agile Requirements and Estimation

Agile requirements and estimation is a huge but important topic. This section covers some of the most important topics here, but there are a lot of ways you can manage requirements and estimates. If you want to master this subject, there are several training modules you can take and books to read. A good starting point is to visit www.scrum.org or www.scrumalliance.com and see what they currently suggest.

Most of the agile planning and estimation tips and tricks in this chapter come from the agile community but aren't specific to Scrum. Scrum really doesn't tell you how to do specific things like planning, estimation, and so on. Scrum is the process framework or process method you use for running your agile projects. However, Scrum works very well with the concepts we look at next.

## Requirements

In agile projects, you usually represent requirements in something called *user stories*. These can be looked at as fluffy requirements—a bit like use cases. You write user stories like this:

> As a <type of user> I want <some functionality> so I may have <some business value>.

One example could be

> As a manager I want my consultants to be able to send in expense reports through the Internet so that I can be more efficient in my expense report process.

Figure 3-6 shows how Microsoft has implemented a user story into the work item type Product Backlog Item in Microsoft Team Foundation Server (TFS). The terminology is a little different from the previous description, but it works.

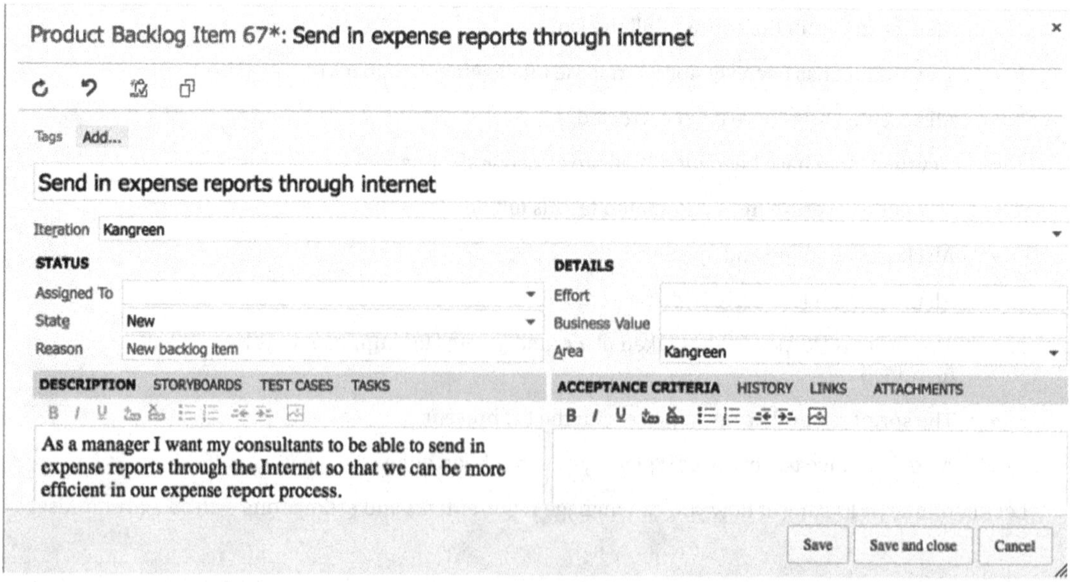

*Figure 3-6.* The user story implementation in the Scrum template Microsoft provides with TFS

User stories capture requirements at a high level and aren't tangled up with detailed functions or implementation details. The details and non-functional requirements are instead captured as acceptance criteria for the user story. Based on these acceptance criteria, you can develop acceptance tests at the same time you write the requirements.

The DoD is also important here because it describes other important requirements that all user stories need to fulfill before they're done.

So, how can you begin gathering requirements before you start a project? POs should use any method they think is suitable. We often use story-writing workshops where important stakeholders, end users, business analysts, experienced developers, and others participate to brainstorm the user stories they can think of. During such a workshop, you focus on the big picture and don't dive into details. These big user stories are often called *epics* because they're large and not broken down yet.

But don't you need to find all requirements at the beginning? No. And that is what makes agile so great. The agile concept builds on the fact that you acknowledge that you don't know and can't know all the requirements early in the project. New requirements and changes to early requirements will pop up throughout the process, and that's okay. The agile approach takes care of this for you. You start with what you have initially, and you continue handling requirements throughout the project. The short version is that you get started right a way and are aware that changes and new requirements will come along.

When the initial requirements are finished, you have the embryo of the product backlog. However, before you can prioritize and estimate these user stories, you need to perform a risk assessment so you can get a grip on the risks associated with each and every one of them. A user story with a significant risk associated with it usually takes more effort to finish and should probably be done early in development.

## Estimation

To know how much effort is involved with a user story, you need to estimate it. The sum of all initial estimates gives you a (very) rough estimate of how much time the entire project may take. But because you know things usually change over time, you don't consider this estimate written in stone.

You have what you need to do estimation: you know the requirements, you have a DoD, and you have acceptance criteria. In the agile world, it's recommended that you estimate time in something called *story points*. Story points aren't an exact size—instead, they're relative.

Here is an easy example we use when running agile training. Take four animals—let's say a cat, a pig, a zebra, and an elephant. Without being a zoologist, most people can say that the pig is three times the size of the cat, the zebra is twice the size of a pig, and the elephant is maybe four times the size of the zebra. If you have a couple of people sit down and discuss these animal sizes, you can pretty soon come up with an agreement about their relative sizes.

The same goes for user stories. Most developers can agree pretty quickly about the relative size of user stories. User story A is twice as big as user story B, and so on. You don't need to be very experienced with the details of each user story to reach this agreement. Novice developers usually end up with the same estimates as experienced ones. Keep in mind that you aren't talking exact time yet, only relative size.

The most common scale for expressing story points is a modified Fibonacci scale. This scale follows the sequence 1, 2, 3, 5, 8, 13, 20, 40, 100.

Often, teams use a technique called *planning poker* when making estimates. Each player has a deck of cards containing the numbers from the modified Fibonacci scale. Here is how planning poker goes:

1. The PO/Scrum master (SM) reads the first user story.

2. The team members briefly consider the user story and select a card each, without showing it to the others.

3. The team members show their cards at the same time.

4. If the result varies much, the people with the highest and lowest cards explain their reasoning.

5.   After a short discussion, the team plays again.

6.   When consensus is reached (or the team members are only one step apart), you're finished.

7.   If the team still disagrees, you pick the highest value.

But what about time? How do you get down to time? You need to know several things to estimate time. The first is *team capacity*. Consider the following when calculating team capacity:

- How long is the sprint?

- How many working days are available in the sprint?

- How many days does each team member work during the sprint? Consider planned vacation or other days off, planned meetings, and so on.

- Deduct the time for sprint planning, review, and retrospective meetings.

The result is the capacity before drag (*drag* is waste time or unknown activities). You should measure drag in each sprint, but at the initial planning it's hard to know how much to include. The longer the project, the more accurate the drag. If you don't know from experience what the drag is, 25% is a good landmark; included in this is 10% backlog grooming.

Now you have the available number of hours in the sprint, and you can connect points and time. You need to know the *team velocity*, which is the number of story points the team can handle in a sprint. Initially this is impossible to know. The easiest way to figure it out is to perform a sprint planning meeting and create a theoretical team velocity. At this meeting, the team breaks down a user story into manageable tasks—and this is where time becomes interesting. During this meeting, the team estimates tasks in hours so they can plan the sprint and decide how many user stories they can take on. The team usually does this as follows:

1.   Estimate the first user story in detail.

2.   Break down what the team needs to do to deliver the story.

3.   Estimate hours for each activity and summarize.

4.   Deduct the summary from the available time the team has in the sprint.

5.   Is there still time left?

6.   If so, take a new user story and repeat the process until no time is left.

7.   Summarize the number of story points from the stories included in the sprint.

Now you have a theoretical velocity.

At this point you can make a rough time plan for the entire project (at this point). This is good input for the POs in their discussions with stakeholders, and also for ROI calculations.

The sprint planning process continues throughout the project, and the theoretical velocity can soon be replaced with one based on experience.

# Backlog

When the initial user stories are in place and estimated with story points, the PO can begin prioritizing the backlog. In Scrum, this is called *ordering the backlog*. Based on the business needs, the PO makes sure the order of the backlog reflects what the business wants. In Figure 3-7, you can see a backlog in Visual Studio Team Services. Usually we do a rough estimate for each backlog item and then a velocity planning. After that, we can see what backlog items should be completed during which sprint.

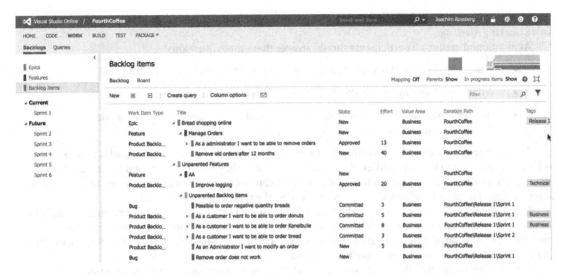

*Figure 3-7.* *A sample backlog in Visual Studio Team Services*

The PO needs to keep the backlog in good shape throughout the project. This means it needs to be ordered. It also needs fine granularity at the top (perhaps three or four sprints down the list) and rougher granularity further down. Keeping the backlog in your ALM toolset gives you the benefit of visibility and traceability. In the best of all worlds, you can link backlog items to code, check-ins, builds, and so on, giving you good traceability.

The PO can also start to look at release planning at this point. It's important to get an overview of coming releases, especially if you have a larger project. Release planning can be done on the epics (the larger user stories). A good approach is to look for themes among the user stories. What could be useful to release at the same time? If you find such features, you can make a theme from them and plan the theme for a certain release.

When this is done, you can also do a very rough time estimate on the releases—and suddenly you also have a rough time plan for the entire project.

Now you have as much information as you could possibly ask for this early in a project. The next step is the sprint planning meeting, when the team members (as you saw earlier) select the backlog items they feel they can commit to during the sprint.

## During the Sprint

During the sprint, you use several important meetings to inspect and adapt your process. We already covered the sprint planning meeting, which takes place at the start of each sprint. But there are other meetings as well, all important to the agile team.

## Daily Stand-Up

The daily stand-up is a meeting that takes place every day during the sprint. This is primarily a developer team meeting and is used to provide status updates to the team members. As the name suggests, this is a stand-up meeting: this comes from the practice of having attendees stand at a meeting because the discomfort of standing for long periods helps keep the meeting short.

The daily stand-ups are kept short, at around 15 minutes, so participants should be reminded that it isn't a working meeting.

As mentioned earlier, all participants should answer these three questions:

- What did I do yesterday that helped the development team meet the sprint goal?

- What will I do today to help the development team meet the sprint goal?

- Do I see any impediment that prevents me or the development team from meeting the sprint goal?

Though it may not be practical to limit all discussion to these three questions, the goal is to stick as closely as possible to them. If further discussions are needed, they should be scheduled for after the meeting. For instance, when team members ask for short clarifications and brief statements, they should try to remember that they should talk about those more after the meeting.

One of the important features of the daily stand-up is that it's intended to be a communication meeting for team members and not a status update for management or other stakeholders. However, it can be valuable for POs to participate in the meeting so they can catch any issues they need to get involved in. This can remove the need for other status meetings afterward.

The meeting is usually held at the same time and place every working day. All team members are encouraged to attend, but the meetings aren't postponed if some team members aren't present.

This practice also promotes closer working relationships with its frequency, need for follow-up conversations, and short duration, which in turn results in a higher rate of knowledge transfer—a much more active result than a typical status meeting.

# Sprint Review

Once the sprint has come to an end, you hold another important meeting: the sprint review. At this meeting, the development team shows the result of what they did during the sprint. They show only the potentially shippable increments of software that they finished during the sprint. Typically this is accomplished using a demo.

Most often the PO, the development team, management, customers, and developers from other projects participate in the sprint review. During the meeting, the project is assessed against the sprint goal determined during the sprint planning meeting. Ideally the team has completed each product backlog item brought into the sprint, but it's more important that the team achieves the overall goal of the sprint.

If some PBIs aren't finished during the sprint, they're put back on the project backlog, and the PO needs to prioritize them for the coming sprint.

# Sprint Retrospective

The most important meeting takes place after the sprint review. This meeting is often the last thing that happens in a sprint and is called the sprint retrospective. It's an opportunity for the team to learn from mistakes by inspecting the sprint and adapting to the results of the inspection. No matter how good a Scrum team is, there are always opportunities to improve. A good Scrum team constantly looks for improvement opportunities, and the team should set aside a brief, dedicated period at the end of each sprint to deliberately reflect on how it's doing and to find ways to improve. Hence the sprint retrospective.

Participants in this meeting should be the development team, the SM, and the PO. Set aside about an hour for this meeting.

There are many ways to do a sprint retrospective. One way is to let the team come up with what was good and what was bad during the sprint. Note these items on a board, and then select (by voting) a number of topics (three to five) from the bad side. Then create action plans for how to improve on them.

Another way is a start-stop-continue meeting. Using this approach, each team member is asked to identify specific things that the team should

- Start doing
- Stop doing
- Continue doing

After an initial list of ideas has been brainstormed, team members proceed and create action plans for how to improve on the "stop doing" issues At the end of the sprint, the next retrospective is often begun by reviewing the list of things selected for attention in the prior retrospective.

Now that you have seen how Scrum is supposed to work, I want to discuss some other agile methodologies that are very commonly used. Scrum is a great process (or rather framework), but it is not the best choice for all organizations or projects.

# Kanban

We'd like to present another method that is usually mentioned with the agile frameworks. *Kanban* is very popular in many organizations and is used by one of our customers today. Even though our preferred project-management method is Scrum for development projects, we realize that Scrum isn't perfect in every situation. Scrum can be scary in the sense that it requires major changes in the way people work in their organizations. It can be hard to implement Scrum fully because humans seem to have an inherent resistance to change. And if you don't have management with you, it's even harder to implement. Wouldn't it be great if you could find a process that was agile but that made it possible for you to make the changes gradually?

Operations can also be difficult to perform using Scrum. Think about this situation for a moment. Let's assume you have three-week sprints for your operations team. One week into a sprint, you suddenly realize that there is a bug in the system that affects production. This bug needs to be fixed right away, so you write a backlog item and present it to the product owner. You need to bring it to the next sprint planning meeting, two weeks from now. Then it will take three weeks for the bug to be fixed, because you have three-week sprints. In the worst case, you'll have to wait five weeks before the fix is available for deployment.

Of course, this is a rare situation. There are obviously ways to handle this better using Scrum. You could, for instance, always have a product backlog item (PBI) of 10% of your available time set aside for bug fixes, and put this PBI at the top of your sprint backlog, allowing you to work on bugs as they're discovered. But we still don't think Scrum is optimal for operations work. This is why we started to look at Kanban.

The name *Kanban* comes from the Japanese word for *signboard*. Kanban goes back to the early days of the Toyota production system. Between 1940 and 1950, Taiichi Ohno developed kanbans to control production between processes and to implement just-in-time (JIT) manufacturing at Toyota manufacturing plants in Japan. The *Kanban method* was developed by David J. Anderson and is an approach to an incremental, evolutionary process as well as systems change for organizations.[10] By using a work-in-progress limited pull system as the core mechanism, it exposes system operation (or process) problems. In such a pull system, tasks that are to be performed are pulled into the workflow, like when you pull a PBI into the sprint backlog. But you can only pull a task into the workflow when there is free capacity to handle the task. It also stimulates collaboration to continuously improving the system.

---

[10]David J. Anderson, *Agile Management for Software Engineering: Applying the Theory of Constraints for Business Results* (Prentice Hall, 2003), and *Kanban: Successful Evolutionary Change for your Technology Business* (Blue Hole Press, 2010).

The Kanban method has three basic principles:[11]

- Start with what you do now.
- Agree to pursue incremental, evolutionary change.
- Respect the current process, roles, responsibilities, and titles.

Let's take a closer look at these.

## Start With What You Do Now

The Kanban method doesn't prescribe a specific set of roles or process steps. There is no such thing as the Kanban Software Development Process or the Kanban Project Management Method. The Kanban method starts with the roles and processes you have and stimulates continuous, incremental, and evolutionary changes to your system. This is the thing we like the best about Kanban. It allows you to continue using what you've invested in; the biggest difference is that you can implement big improvements to the existing process without worrying employees.

## Agree to Pursue Incremental, Evolutionary Change

The organization (or team) must agree that continuous, incremental, and evolutionary change is the way to make system improvements and make them stick. Sweeping changes may seem more effective, but more often than not they fail due to resistance and fear in the organization. The Kanban method encourages continuous, small, incremental, and evolutionary changes to your current system.

## Respect the Current Process, Roles, Responsibilities, and Titles

It's likely that the organization currently has some elements that work acceptably and are worth preserving. You must also seek to drive out fear in order to facilitate future change. By agreeing to respect current roles, responsibilities, and job titles, you eliminate initial fears. This should enable you to gain broader support for your Kanban initiative. Presenting Kanban as compared to an alternative, more sweeping approach that would lead to changes in titles, roles, and responsibilities and perhaps the wholesale removal of certain positions may help individuals realize the benefits of this approach.

## The Five Core Properties

David Anderson, in his book *Kanban*, identified five core properties that are part of each successful implementation of the Kanban method:

- Visualize the workflow.
- Limit work in progress (WIP).
- Manage flow.
- Make process policies explicit.
- Improve collaboratively.

Let's look at these and learn what they mean.

---

[11]*Taiichi Ohno, Norman Bodek, Toyota Production System: Beyond Large-Scale Production* (Productivity Press, 1988).

# Visualize the Workflow

The knowledge work of today hides its workflow in information systems. In order to understand how work works, so to speak, it's important to visualize the flow of work. The right changes are harder to perform if you don't understand the workflow. One common way to visualize the workflow is by using a wall with cards and columns, called a *Kanban board*. The columns on the card wall represent the different states or steps in the workflow, and the cards represent the feature/story/task/result of the workflow, usually referred to as *work items*.

What is great is that you use the steps of your existing workflow—you don't need to enforce a new way of working that dramatically changes the current approach. You basically place the Kanban process on top of what you have, and visualize this flow. This often feels more comfortable to co-workers and makes them more positive about the small changes you're imposing on them.

Figure 3-8 shows the Kanban board that is used to visualize the flow. But wait, some may say: isn't this just like a Scrum board, shown in Figure 3-9? Yes, but there is one significant difference if you compare the figures closely. Above each Kanban board column is a number that identifies the WIP limit. This takes us to the next core property: limit work in progress.

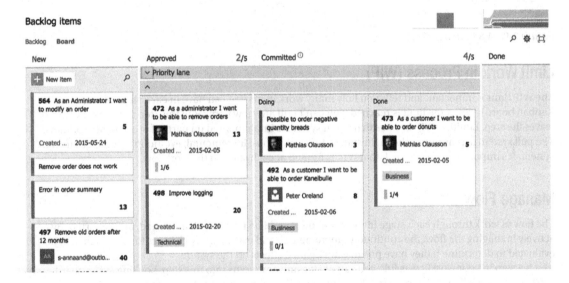

*Figure 3-8. A Kanban board*

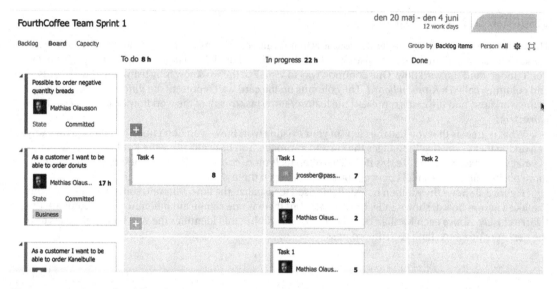

*Figure 3-9.* *A Scrum board*

## Limit Work in Process (WIP)

The WIP limit is important and tells you how many work items you can have in each step (column on the Kanban board). When the limit is reached, you can't pull any new items into this step until a work item leaves the step. Limiting WIP implies that a pull system is implemented on parts of or all of the workflow. The pull system acts as one of the main stimuli for continuous, incremental, evolutionary changes to your system. It's important, even critical, that WIP is limited at each stage in the workflow.

## Manage Flow

The flow of work through each stage in the workflow should be monitored, measured, and reported. By actively managing the flow, the continuous, incremental, and evolutionary changes to the system can be evaluated to determine if they have positive or negative effects on the system.

If a step in your workflow is full, you can't bring any new items into this step. Looking at the board, you can easily see if there is a bottleneck in your flow. If you discover that all columns to the right of the development step on your board are empty, but the development step is full (see Figure 3-10), this means something is stopping development, and people working on development can't finalize their work. You should use idle resources to try to help the developers solve what is stopping them so you can restart the flow and begin pulling new work items into the steps. By having this visibility, you can manage your flow and make sure you handle problems as they arise.

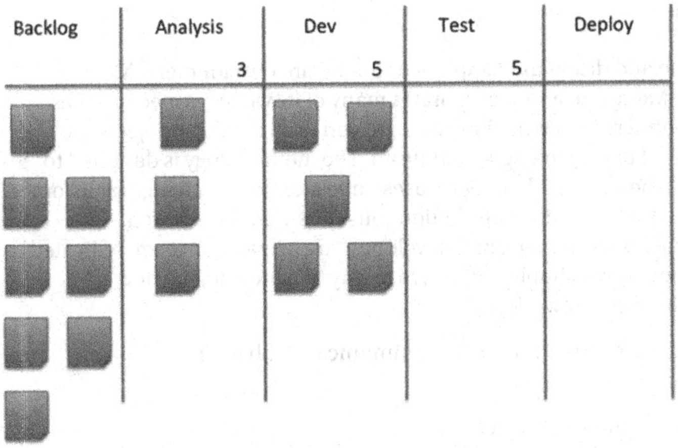

| Backlog | Analysis | | Dev | | Test | | Deploy |
|---------|----------|---|-----|---|------|---|--------|
| | | 3 | | 5 | | 5 | |

*Figure 3-10.* *A bottleneck in the flow has been discovered*

## Make Process Policies Explicit

It's often hard to improve, or even start a discussion of improving, a process until the mechanism of the process is made explicit. Without an explicit understanding of how things work and how work is actually done, any discussion of problems often seems subjective or emotional. To get a more rational, empirical, and objective discussion of issues, explicit understanding is important. This will most likely lead to consensus around improvement suggestions.

## Improve Collaboratively (Using Models and the Scientific Method)

Kanban encourages small, continuous, incremental, and evolutionary changes that stick. David Anderson also discovered this was very effective. Resistance to change, as we've mentioned, is easier to overcome if the steps are small and each step has a great payback. Teams that have a shared understanding of theories about work, workflow, process, and risk are more likely to be able to build a common understanding of a problem and thereby suggest improvement actions that can be agreed on by consensus. The Kanban method proposes a scientific approach to be used to implement continuous, incremental, and evolutionary changes. But the method doesn't prescribe a specific scientific method to use.

## Common Models Used to Understand Work in Kanban

Some common models are often used with Kanban to understand how work actually works. We don't go into these in detail, but include them for reference:

- The Theory of Constraints (the study of bottlenecks)

- The System of Profound Knowledge (a study of variation and how it affects processes)

- Lean Economic Model (based on the concepts of "waste" [or muda, muri, and mura])

# Extreme Programming

Extreme Programming (XP) is a deliberate and disciplined approach to software development. XP, like Scrum, was a direct outcome of the Agile Manifesto and incorporates many of its values. Aspects of these models had been in the minds of their founders for a long time, though, and used in many projects. XP stresses customer satisfaction, an important part of the Agile Manifesto. The methodology is designed to deliver the software the customer needs, when it's needed. XP focuses on responding to changing customer requirements, even late in the lifecycle, so that customer satisfaction (business value) is assured.

XP also emphasizes teamwork. Managers, customers, and developers are all part of a team dedicated to delivering high-quality software. XP implements a simple and effective way to handle teamwork.

There are four ways XP improves software teamwork:

- *Communication:* It's essential that XP programmers communicate with their customers and fellow programmers.

- *Simplicity:* The design should be simple and clean.

- *Feedback:* Feedback is supplied by testing the software from the first day of development. Testing is done by writing the unit tests before even writing the code. This is called TDD, and it is becoming a frequently used practice in many projects, not only agile ones. You see later how Team Foundation Server (TFS) implements TDD.

- *Courage:* The software should be delivered to the customers as early as possible, and a goal is to implement changes as suggested. XP stresses that developers should be able to courageously respond to changing requirements and technology based on this foundation.

RUP has use cases, and XP has *user stories*. These serve the same purpose as use cases, but they aren't the same. They're used to create time estimates for the project and also replace bulky requirements documentation. The stakeholders (managers, end users, project sponsors, and so on) are responsible for writing the user stories, which should be about things the system needs to do for them. Stakeholders write stories because they're the ones who know what functionality they need and desire—developers rarely have this kind of information. Each user story consists of about three sentences of text written by the stakeholder in the stakeholder's own terminology, without any of the technical software jargon that a developer may use.

Another important issue is that XP stresses the importance of delivering working software in increments so the customer can give feedback as early as possible. By expecting that this will happen, developers are ready to implement changes.

The last topic we want to highlight with XP is *pair programming*. All code to be included in a production release is created by two people working together at a single computer. This approach increases software quality without impacting time to delivery. Although we've never had the benefit of trying this ourselves, co-workers we've spoken to who have used pair programming are confident that it adds as much functionality as two developers working separately. The difference is that quality is much higher. Laurie Williams of the University of Utah in Salt Lake City has shown that pair programmers are 15% slower than two independent individual programmers, but "error-free" code increases from 70% to 85%.[12] In our opinion, this more than makes up for the decrease in speed.

---

[12]Laurie Williams et al., *Pair Programming Illuminated* (Addison-Wesley, 2003).

We can make a reference to my old job as an assistant air-traffic controller here. Many are the times he sat in the tower when airplane traffic was so heavy that he needed help keeping track of every airplane. Although this isn't the same thing, the fact remains that two pairs of eyes see more than one pair—and this is what makes pair programming so attractive.

To learn more about extreme programming, we encourage you to visit `www.extremeprogramming.org/`.

# Scaling Scrum

What happens if you have more team members than can fit on a Scrum team (seven plus/minus two people)? What if 90 people are involved in the project? Can Scrum scale to handle this? According to Mike Cohn, in an article on the Scrum Alliance web site,[13] you can use a process called *Scrum of Scrums*:

The Scrum of Scrums meeting is an important technique in scaling Scrum to large project teams. These meetings allow clusters of teams to discuss their work, focusing especially on areas of overlap and integration. Imagine a perfectly balanced project comprising seven teams each with seven team members. Each of the seven teams would conduct (simultaneously or sequentially) its own daily Scrum meeting. Each team would then designate one person to also attend a Scrum of Scrums meeting. The decision of who to send should belong to the team. Usually the person chosen should be a technical contributor on the team—a programmer, tester, database administrator, designer, and so on—rather than a product owner or Scrum master.

By using this technique, you can scale Scrum infinitely, at least in theory.

But there are other ways to scale Scrum and agile as well. We will take a look at two of them here:

- Scaled Agile Framework (SAFe)

- Scaled Professional Scrum (SPS)

# SAFe

Dean Leffingwell's SAFe, the Scaled Agile Framework (Figure 3-11), is designed by Scaled Agile, Inc. SAFe allows large organizations to move toward a more agile way of working. And by large I mean more than 1,000 people in IT, and more than 250 in software development. But SAFe can be just as effective for teams of 50–100 people.

---

[13]Mike Cohn, "Advice on Conducting the Scrum of Scrums Meeting," May 7, 2007, `www.scrumalliance.org/articles/46-advice-on-conducting-the-scrum-of-scrums-meeting`.

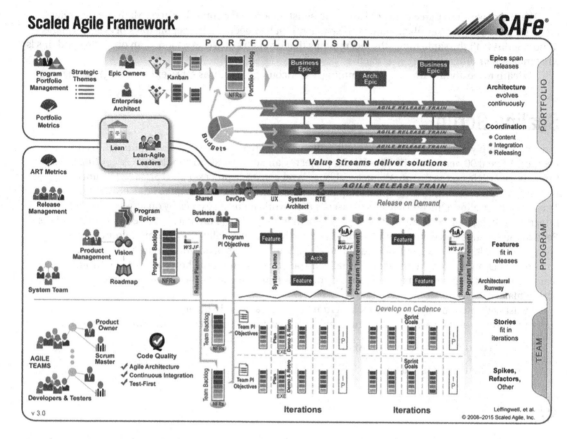

***Figure 3-11.*** *SAFe—The big picture*

The debate on how best to scale up the Scrum (and the agile methodology) have sometimes been high. Especially how to do this in large organizations, which often operate their projects in an application environment with several subprojects and many Scrum teams. Much debate has concerned how to best synchronize the development work with multiple teams or subprojects running simultaneously and where people work toward a common goal. Scaled Agile Framework (SAFe) has been developed in order to benefit these organizations and the difficulties they may encounter.

In SAFe the synchronization occurs at many different levels. Roles and activities are organized around something called an Agile Release Trains (ART). These trains depart on a predetermined schedule that gives an opportunity to plan and synchronize releases on a program level.

The agile development team in SAFe consists of cross-functional individuals (8-10) who have the ability and confidence to define, build, and test a solution or system in an iterative workflow. The team consists of developers, testers, a Scrum master, a product owner, and any other necessary skills for the team to succeed in delivering business value. Because teams often use XP techniques, they are often known as a SAFe ScrumXP team.

Several teams create what SAFe calls a release train, which organizes around a program. An ART can have multiple ScrumXP teams, which together build the solution. Each team has its own backlog, which is an excerpt of the overall program backlog. This places high demands on how to synchronize data and work between the team. This occurs in different ways.

ScrumXP teams are the force behind a release train and to sync with other teams all product owners meet in an expanded product ownership team. Additionally, each team's iterations sync with the other teams to coordinate the construction of the solution.

A further option to sync the teams with each other is through the Scrum of Scrum meetings. These are meetings where representatives of the different ScrumXP teams meet. They are held at least every week but more often when necessary.

In SAFe, the team's work is synchronized on several different levels in order to maintain a good and stable pace and keep the solution together at a higher level than just the team level. You can find more information about SAFe at http://www.scaledagileframework.com.

SAFe is one way to scale Scrum. We will now take a look at another way that originates from Ken Schwaber and Scrum.org.

# Scaled Professional Scrum (SPS)

In Scaled Professional Scrum, a Nexus (nexusguide.org) is an exoskeleton that rests on top of multiple scrum teams when they are combined to create an integrated increment. Nexus is consistent with Scrum and its parts will be familiar to those who have worked on Scrum projects. The difference is that this method pays more attention to dependencies and interoperation between scrum teams, delivering one "done" integrated increment at least every sprint.

The result can be an effective development group of up to around 90 people. Scrum.org recommends 3-9 Scrum teams with 3-9 developers. This includes the Nexus Integration Team. For larger initiatives, the Nexus becomes a unit of scale. This is called Nexus+, a unification of more than one Nexus.

As displayed in Figure 3-12, Nexus consists of:

- *Roles:* A new role, the Nexus Integration Team, exists to coordinate, coach, and supervise the application of Nexus and the operation of Scrum so the best outcomes are derived. The Nexus Integration Team consists of the Product Owner, a Scrum master, and 3-9 developers.

- *Artifacts:* All scrum teams use the same, single product backlog. As the product backlog items are refined and made ready, indicators of which team will do the work inside a sprint are made visual. A new artifact, the Nexus sprint backlog, exists to raise this transparency during the sprint. All Scrum teams maintain their individual sprint backlogs.

- *Events:* Events are appended to, placed around, or replace (in the case of the sprint review) regular Scrum events to augment them. As modified, they serve both the overall effort of all Scrum teams in the Nexus, and each individual team. Backlog refinement has become a proper event as well. This is an important practice for single teams but at scale it becomes mandatory.

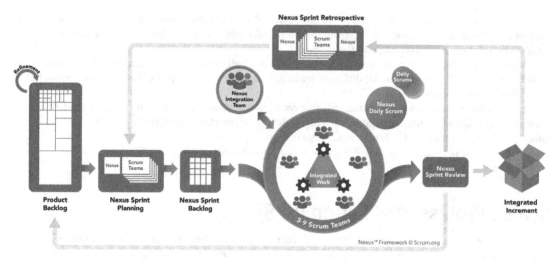

**Figure 3-12.** *The Nexus framework (nexusguide.org)*

All work in a Nexus may be done by all members of the Scrum teams, as cross-functional members of the Nexus. Based on dependencies, the teams may select the most appropriate members to do specific work.

- *Refine the product backlog:* The product backlog needs to be decomposed so that dependencies are identified and removed or minimized. Product backlog items are refined into thinly sliced pieces of functionality and the team likely to do the work should be identified as early as possible.

- *Nexus sprint planning:* Appropriate representatives from each Scrum team meet to discuss and review the refined product backlog. They select product backlog items for each team. Each Scrum team then plans its own sprint, interacting with other teams as appropriate. The outcome is a set of sprint goals that align with the overarching Nexus goal, each Scrum team's sprint backlog, and a single Nexus sprint backlog. The Nexus sprint backlog makes the Scrum team's selected product backlog items and any dependencies transparent.

- *Development work:* All teams develop software, frequently integrating their work into a common environment that can be tested to ensure that the integration is done.

- *Nexus daily Scrum:* Appropriate representatives from each Scrum development team meet daily to identify if any integration issues exist. If identified, this information is transferred back to each Scrum development team's daily Scrum. Scrum development teams then use their daily Scrum to create a plan for the day, being sure to address the integration issues raised during the Nexus daily scrum.

- *Nexus sprint review:* All teams meet with the appropriate stakeholders to review the integrated increment. Stakeholder feedback may result in adjustments to the product backlog.

- *Nexus Sprint Retrospective:* Appropriate representatives from each Scrum team meet to identify shared challenges. Then, each Scrum team holds individual sprint retrospectives. Appropriate representatives from each team meet again to discuss any actions needed based on shared challenges to provide bottom-up intelligence.

SAFe and SPS take different approaches to scaling Scrum. I have seen some efforts to use SAFe at some larger customers but I still wait for long-term results in order to evaluate them better.

# How Agile Maps to ALM

According to Forrester, agile adoption has brought about significant support for ALM practices.[14] The agile way of working using frequent inspection and adaption coupled with increased delivery cadence has made teams more disciplined in their way of working. When agile was introduced, many people thought the opposite would be true; but reality has proved them wrong.

What parts of agile map to the ALM process? Let's look at what Forrester says.

## Agile Captures Task-Based Work

Daily stand-up meetings allow team members to report progress against their tasks. As you've seen in this chapter, the PBIs are broken down into tasks during sprint planning, and each task is reported on, aggregating the results to the original PBI. Using digital tooling for this—such as Mylyn from Tasktop and TFS from Microsoft—allows you to capture effort, time, and other metadata, which can provide valuable insight into the real progress of your software development.

## Increased Frequency of Inspection

The iterative approach to development improves the frequency of inspection. During each sprint, you have project inspection at each daily stand-up. At the end of a sprint, during the sprint retrospective, you define what you've done well and what needs to be improved. This improves the feedback loop and, together with better visibility for reporting and traceability, has far-reaching implications for ALM.

## Many Tools Collect Much Information

Many agile teams use tools that help them collect build and integration information in their continuous integration flow. This improves visibility into the build process as well as traceability, because the tools often allow the team to see which requirements, work items, and tests each build included.

---

■ **Note** "Continuous Integration is a software development practice where members of a team integrate their work frequently, usually each person integrates at least daily, leading to multiple integrations per day. Each integration is verified by an automated build (including test) to detect integration errors as quickly as possible. Many teams find that this approach leads to significantly reduced integration problems and allows a team to develop cohesive software more rapidly." —Martin Fowler[15]

---

[14]Dave West, "The Time Is Right For ALM 2.0+," October 19, 2010, Forrester Research, www.forrester.com/ The+Time+Is+Right+For+ALM+20/fulltext/-/E-RES56832?objectid=RES56832.
[15]Martin Fowler, "Continuous Integration," May 1, 2006, http://martinfowler.com/articles/ continuousIntegration.html.

## Test Artifacts Are Important

Agile teams often use test-driven development and increase the importance of test artifacts. Business analysts and quality assurance practices are converging, which is something that agile methods encourage. Agile's emphasis on the definition of *done* and frequent inspection increases the desire to link work items with test plans and cases. The result is that agile teams create simpler requirements but see higher integration with test assets.

## Agile Teams Plan Frequently

Agile teams plan more frequently than traditional teams. Planning takes place when creating work items, during sprint planning, during daily stand-ups, during backlog grooming, and so on.

As a result, agile teams have more information about their projects, such as estimates, actual results, and predictions. This enables ALM to move center stage, because planning activities are an important management component of an ALM application.

# Summary

The goal of this chapter has been to introduce agile concepts. We focused on Scrum and Kanban since they are so commonly used. We looked at the details of Scrum so you can understand why the agile approach maps so well to the ALM process.

We also looked at two ways to scale Scrum and agility in order to become more agile in larger projects or larger organizations.

Using agile techniques can help you with visibility, traceability, and collaboration.

# CHAPTER 4

■ ■ ■

# Work Items and Process Templates

This chapter looks at the heart and soul of projects in TFS or VSTS. You will see how all projects build on a process template or just process, as Microsoft calls them these days. The process defines all aspects of your projects including work items types, workflow states, and so on.

## ALM Revisited

Having traceability in the ALM processes is key to the successful delivery and maintenance of your applications and systems. Chapter 1 showed that traceability is one of the three cornerstones in a successful ALM solution.

- *Traceability of relationships between artifacts*: Traceability can be a major cost driver in any enterprise if it's not done correctly. There must be a way of tracing the requirements all the way to delivered code—through architect models, design models, build scripts, unit tests, test cases, and so on. Practices such as test-driven development and configuration management can help, and these can be automated and supported by TFS.

- *Automation of high-level processes*: There are approval processes to control handoffs between analysis and design. There are other handoffs between build, deployment, testing, and so on. Much of this is done manually in many projects, and ALM stresses the importance of automating these tasks for a more effective and less time-consuming process.

- *Visibility into the progress of development efforts*: Many managers and stakeholders have limited visibility into the progress of development projects. Their visibility often comes from steering group meetings during which the project manager goes over the current situation. Other interest groups such as project members may also have limited visibility of the whole project even though they are part of it. This often occurs because reporting is hard to do and can involve a lot of manual work. Daily status reports can quite simply take too much time and effort to produce, for example, especially when we have information in many repositories.

The next section discusses in more detail how work items in TFS can help you accomplish traceability in your projects and organizations.

© Joachim Rossberg 2016

J. Rossberg, *Agile Project Management using Team Foundation Server 2015*,

DOI 10.1007/978-1-4842-1870-9_4

# Traceability

Unfortunately we have seen companies that have stopped making changes to their systems just because no one ever knew where a change (or bug fix) might have its impact. This is not a situation any organization wants to end up with. Yet it is quite common.

At the Swedish Road Administration some years ago, a new version of our system suddenly made old bug fixes disappear. The operators at the Traffic Management Center found themselves with no working phones because of an upgrade. This had the potential to make an accident worse than it already was, because the operators communicate with the rescue team and the police using phones. Having communications suddenly stop working can be a matter of life or death.

The vendor of that piece of software did not have control over its different software versions and did not have a good testing strategy. If the vendor had used automated tests, for instance, they would have discovered broken tests for the bug fix when the fix itself was not included in the next release. By checking which work items were associated with the failed test(s), the vendor would have been able to see which of these contained the problem. This would have indicated why they created the test in the first place, so they could have more easily fixed the problem. This traceability would greatly improve their code.

And if they had used a good configuration management process, they would also have had the capability to trace all versions where the bug fix needed to be inserted, so they wouldn't forget to include it in the coming releases.

Work item tracking in TFS can help with traceability so you can avoid such problems. Let's now see how the work item tracking system implements traceability.

## The TFS Work Item Tracking System

Sometimes it seems like we can have tons of Post-its on our monitors and desks—each one containing at least one task we are supposed to do. Often it just isn't possible to track them with a tool. It could be that some tasks are connected with one project, others with another. We could try writing them all down in an Excel sheet and saving that to our computer. But soon we might find that the spreadsheet is located at our laptop, the customer computer, the desktop, at another customer computer, and so on. And we have no idea which one is the current version. This can be a real problem sometimes when we find we have no clue as to which version we should trust.

The same thing is often visible in projects. Project managers have their to-do lists for a project, and they all have their own way of keeping them updated. Let's say a PM uses Excel to keep track of the tasks—the status of tasks, whom they are assigned to, and so on. How can the PM keep the team updated with the latest to-do list? If the PM chooses to e-mail it, chances are that some won't save the new version to disk or will just miss it in the endless stream of e-mails coming into the mailbox. Soon there are various versions floating around, and things are generally a mess.

One way to solve this could be to use a project web site running on Microsoft Office SharePoint Server or some other tool like that. This could help, although you could still be in trouble if people forget to save changes or check in the document after they have updated it.

Another problem may occur if, for example, an Excel sheet is updated by a tester who discovers a bug and changes the status of one entry in the task list to indicate that a developer should look at the task again and solve the bug. How can you alert the developer that the bug exists? You would want this action to take place automatically, right? That would be hard if you used only an Excel sheet. The same thing occurs the other way around. When a developer has fixed a bug, you want the tester to be alerted that the problem has been resolved, so the tester can then check whether the bug can be closed.

What about requirements traceability? If the only place you keep track of the connection between requirements and the code is in a document, how do you know that the document is really updated? Can you trust that information?

Even if you purchase a separate tool to help keep track of tasks, it would still be a separate tool for all categories of team members. There are tools for bug tracking, requirements management, test management, and so on—the list can go on for a while. Chances are that someone will forget to update the tool because it takes too long to open or is too difficult to work in or any other excuse for not doing the update. This could cost the project lots of money and time.

# Work Items

In TFS you have a task-tracking system at your service. The core of this system is represented by the tasks themselves, called work items. A work item can be pretty much what you want it to be. It can be a bug, a requirement of some sort, a general to-do item, and so on. Each work item represents an object that is stored in the Team Foundation Server database. All work items have a unique ID that helps keep track of the places it is referenced (see Figure 4-1).

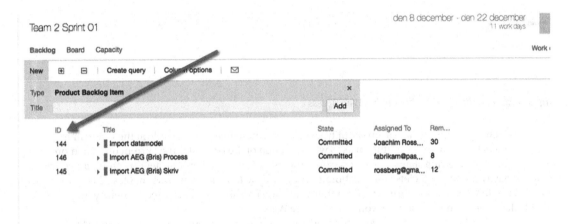

***Figure 4-1.** Each work item has a unique ID*

The ID lets you follow one work item, let's say a requirement, from its creation to its implementation as a piece of executable software (component). Work item IDs are unique across all work item types in all team projects in a project collection. The work item type determines the work item fields that are available for tracking information, defaults defined for each field, and rules and constraints positioned on these fields and other objects that specify the work item workflow. Every change made to a work item field is stored in the work item log, which maintains a historical record of changes (`https://msdn.microsoft.com/en-us/library/vs/alm/work/track/history-and-auditing`).

You can create and modify work items by using Team Explorer, TFS Web, Office Excel, or Office Project. When creating or modifying individual work items, you can work in the work item form, by using Team Explorer or Team Web Access (see Figure 4-2). You can make bulk updates to many work items at a time by using TFS Web, Office Excel, or Office Project.

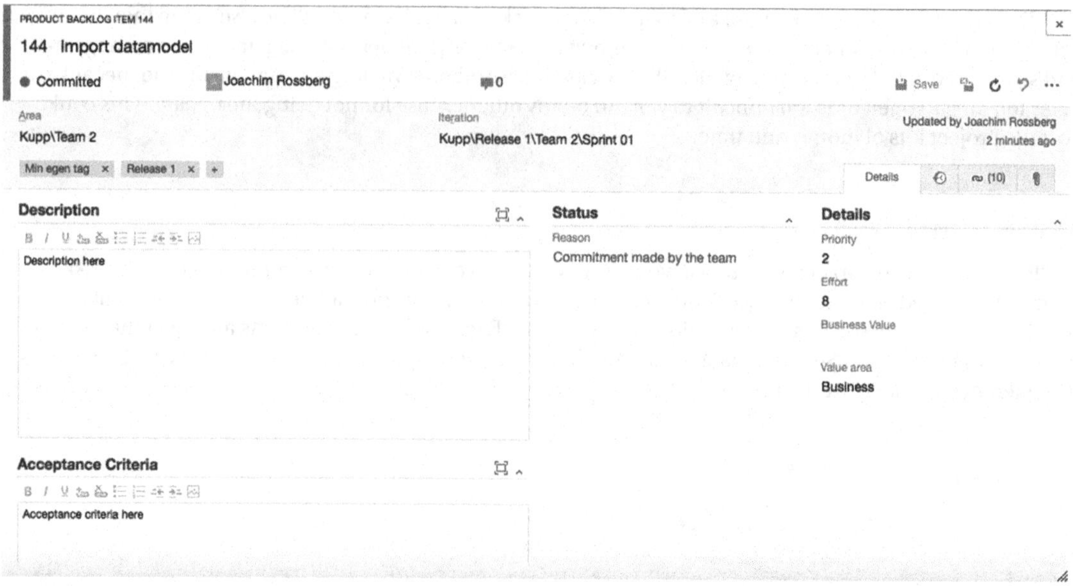

*Figure 4-2.* *Creating a work item using Web Access*

Work items provide a great way to simplify task management in a project while at the same time enabling traceability. No more confusion as to which version of the task list is the current one. No more manual labor for gathering status reports on work progress that are used only at steering group meetings. Now you have a solution that lets you collaborate more easily with your teams and enables all members and stakeholders to view status reports whenever they want. You can also more easily collaborate with people outside the project group by adding work items via the Web.

TFS is so flexible that it lets you tailor the work items as you want them to be. By installing TFS Power Tools, you get an additional menu option called Process Editor under Tools in Visual Studio (see Figure 4-3), which simplifies editing the work items and the whole process as well. From this tool you can modify the work items in the project so they contain new information. Later in this chapter, you will learn more on how you can change your process template, including the work items. If you make a change to the current project (by modifying a work item for example) this affects all new work items you create, but not the existing ones. You only get the change in your current project as well. All new projects created with the same process template will not include these changes, unless you modify the process template on the TFS server.

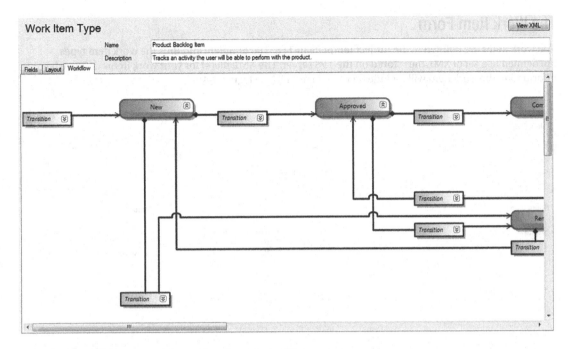

*Figure 4-3. Modifying a work item using the process editor*

The work items can contain information in different fields that define the data to be stored in the work item. This means that each field will have a name and a data type. Data types supported in fields are the primitive data types such as string, integer, and double, as well some complex types such as DateTime, PlainText, HTML, and others. System fields are one example of a field (or more correct, a label for a group of fields) that must be present in every work item type, and they represent the minimal recommended subset of fields that any custom work item template should contain. Having such a common subset allows reusing basic Work Item Query Language (WIQL) queries or reports from predefined templates for your custom templates.

All work items can have different information attached to them. You can have information about whom the work item is assigned to and the status of the work at the moment (for example, a bug could be open, closed, under investigation, resolved, and so on). The State field can be modified (see Figure 4-3) so that each work item type can have its own state mechanism. This is logical because a bug probably goes through different states than a general task goes through, for instance. You can also attach documents to the work item and link one work item to other work items. You can create a hierarchy of work items if you want. Say that you implement a requirement as a work item and this requirement contains many smaller tasks. Then you can have the requirement itself at the top and nest the other requirements below that so you know which work items belong to which requirement.

When a bug is discovered, for instance, you can quickly follow the original requirement by its work item ID and see in which places of the code you might have to make some fixes. You can also see the associated work items so that you can evaluate whether other parts of the code need to be changed as a result of this bug fix.

Because TFS saves information about the work item on the data tier, you can see the history of the work item. You can see who created it, who resolved it, who closed it, and so on. The information in the databases can be used for display on reports, allowing you to tailor these depending on your needs. One report could show the status of all bugs, for instance. Stakeholders can see how many open bugs exist, how many are resolved, and much, much more. It is completely up to you how you choose to use the work items.

For those familiar with and used to working with pivot tables, you can use Excel as well to drill down into the information in the TFS data warehouse. There are people who think it is better to use Excel to directly connect to these tables and who use very detailed information in their reports.

# The Work Item Form

The work items are defined in the project template in TFS. The template and thus the work item types are defined in a set of XML files stored on the TFS server. The XML file(s) for your work items define what information the work item will include on its form in TFS (see Figure 4-4).

*Figure 4-4.* *The bug form in Microsoft Scrum*

As you can see in Figure 4-4, the bug work item type in Microsoft Scrum includes fields for many aspects of the bug. You can assign the bug to a specific person, set its state (status), set its severity, and much more. You can also add a description of the problem and attach files such as screenshots of the bug. There are other options as well, but we will not cover them here.

The fields on the work item form can have properties set for them. You can let a field be read-only, required, automatically populated, and so on. Because you can also change what information is included on this form by editing the XML, you can make it include the information that you want.

We have heard some customers say that they have had problems using the process templates that Microsoft provides because the information required to fill in the forms is not the information they want to track or record. Instead of changing the work item types, they have tried to adapt to the work items. Don't make this mistake! If you need other information besides what is included in the templates, or if you need the information in another way, change the template. That's the whole point of having an open and flexible solution such as TFS. You can adjust the tool to fit your needs. I have, for instance, seen the bug work item that Microsoft uses, and it looks nothing like what is included in any of the templates you get with TFS. Instead Microsoft encourages you to adjust the tool to your needs. This includes adjusting the work items.

# Work Item Traceability

Consider this little example of how you can use work items to increase traceability. We start with a requirement in the form of a user story:

> *"As a manager I want to search expense reports so that I can get an overview of expenses more easily."*

This user story is entered into TFS and TFS assigns an ID to it (Figure 4-5). This ID will follow the work item all through its life.

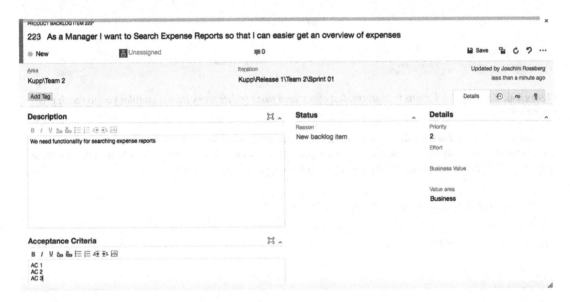

***Figure 4-5.*** *Traceability starts with a work item in TFS*

Figure 4-6 shows how you can associate the work item with test cases, tasks, and other work items. This means that you can get traceability from a requirement to test cases, to storyboards, and to other work items.

***Figure 4-6.*** *Linking work items to features, test cases, and tasks (other work items) enables you to reach great traceability*

You can also do this the other way around. When creating storyboards, test cases, or work items, you can of course link them to a new work item (see Figure 4-7) or to another, existing, work item. This is a huge benefit over keeping this information in our heads or on an Excel spreadsheet.

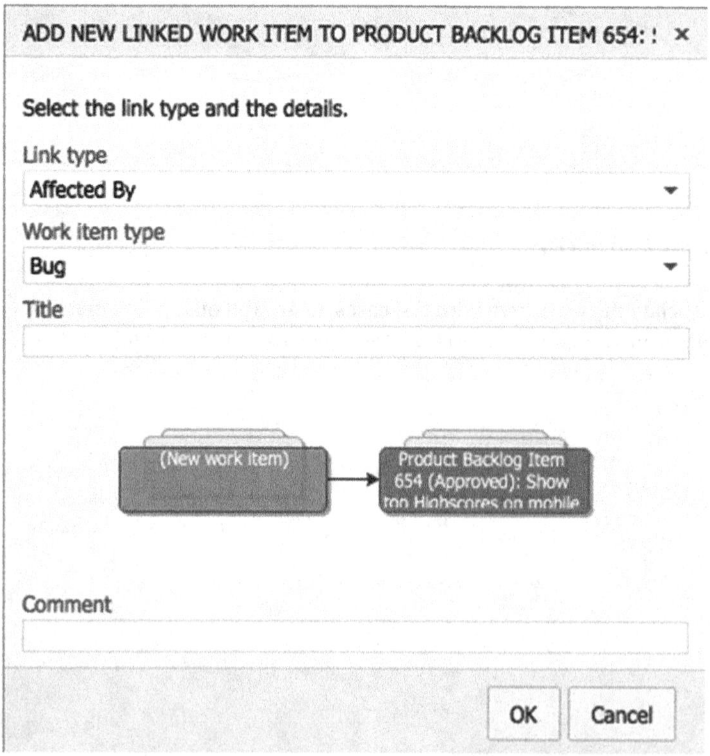

## ADD NEW LINKED WORK ITEM TO PRODUCT BACKLOG ITEM 654: :  ✕

**Select the link type and the details.**

Link type

  Affected By                                                       ▼

Work item type

  Bug                                                       ▼

Title

Comment

                                            OK     Cancel

***Figure 4-7.*** *Linking work items to new or existing work items*

You can also define check-in rules for your developers, which forces them to associate a check-in/changeset with a work item(s), as can be seen in Figure 4-8. There should not be any need for a check-in unless the code change is associated with a work item. You should never make any code changes unless they are required to solve an issue, and this issue should always be documented as a work item.

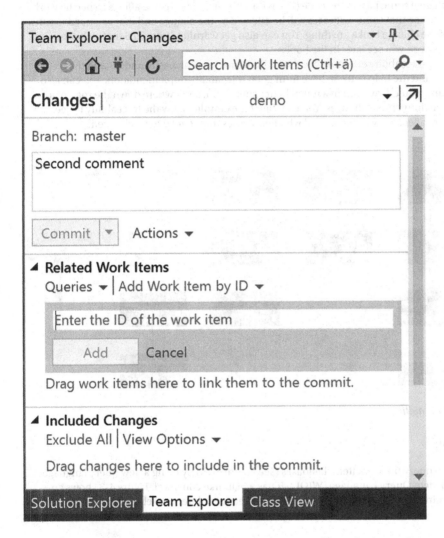

*Figure 4-8.* *Linking a work item to a check-in can be required by a check-in policy*

A changeset in TFS is a logical container into which TFS bundles everything related to a single check-in operation. A changeset consists of:

- Source file and folder revisions (adds, renames, edits, deletes, and moves)
- Related work items (bugs, etc.)
- System metadata (owner, date/time, etc.)
- Check-in notes and comments

By associating a build with a changeset, you can create traceability from the original requirement (user story in this case) to the built executable.

This traceability can help you avoid problems like the ones described in the beginning of the chapter. By using the reporting functionality of TFS, you can quickly see what a work item is associated with and hence know that if you change some part of the code (like with a bug fix), this change affects a specific work item. Knowing this you can see that some test cases will be affected by the change and that you need to run those tests again to see if the change broke anything. You can also get warnings from TFS that a check-in affects certain test cases, as you will see later in the book.

Figure 4-9 shows what traceability can look like. From this figure, you can easily understand the importance of traceability and the help you can have from good traceability implementation. You can also see that this way of working would leave you in a much better spot if you, somewhere down the road of a production system, need to implement changes. You can then for example follow the traceability to see which parts of the code are affected by a change and which test cases might need to be changed.

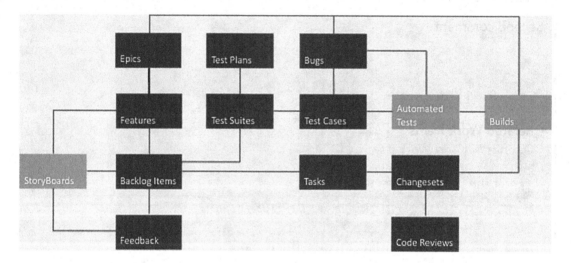

*Figure 4-9.* Work item traceability

## Work Item Queries

In Team Explorer, you can query the work item databases (see Figure 4-10) by using a new query language Microsoft provides: Work Item Query Language (WIQL). It has a SQL-like construct. Figure 4-3 shows an example of a query returning all active bugs, for instance. From Team Explorer or Web Access, you can create new queries or modify existing ones.

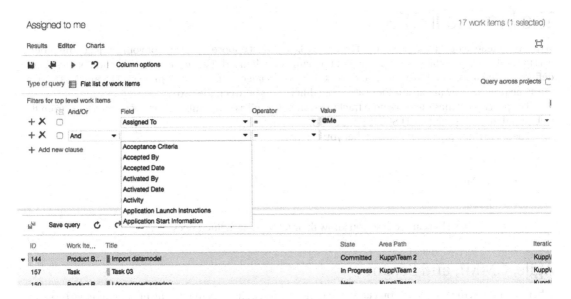

***Figure 4-10.*** *Work item queries in Web Access*

Depending on the process template you use, the work item queries that are supplied differ quite a bit. Microsoft Scrum has different work item queries than the agile template, for instance. When we have used the the agile template in some of my projects, we have found it necessary to add new work item types because the organization needed these for their ALM process. Queries to get information about these new work item types naturally don't exist, so we have had to make these queries ourselves. Some of these queries have been built during the projects when the need arose, and many of these have later been included in the process template so they are now part of all new projects.

## Conclusions on the Work Item Tracking System

The work item tracking system is one of the core components of TFS. This system enables you to create work items, or units of work, and can be used to enable traceability. You can use the work items included with TFS from the beginning, or you can choose to adjust these to your needs, or even create your own work item types. Each work item instance has a unique ID (as you saw earlier in Figure 4-1) that you can attach to the things you do in TFS. This enables you to follow one work item—let's say a requirement, for example—from its creation to its implementation as a piece of executable software (component). You can also associate one work item with others and build a hierarchy of work items.

When a bug is discovered, you can quickly follow the original requirement by its work item ID and see in which places of the code you might have to make some fixes. You can also see the associated work items so that you can evaluate whether other parts of the code also need to be changed as a result of this bug fix.

If you implement a requirement as a work item, you can use the work item ID to track this requirement through source code and to the final build of the executable system. By requiring all developers to add one or more work item IDs to the check-in using a check-in policy, you can enable this traceability.

Our suggestion is that you look closely at the work item types supplied by Microsoft. Then you can decide which of those you can use for yourself and which you might adjust to suit your organization's needs. If none of the ones supplied can be used, you have the capability to create your own work item types. Use this opportunity! Don't adjust your way of working to the Microsoft templates. Adjust TFS to your needs instead.

# The Process in TFS

When you create a new team project in TFS or VSTS, you must choose a process for your project. The process was formerly known as process template but the name has changed. The *process* is a collection of files that defines the features, rules, behaviors, and work items associated with a specific process. TFS and VSTS have the same processes available but there are some differences between the two.

The process defines the work item tracking system as well as other sub-systems you can access from the web portal for a on-premises TFS or through VSTS.

There are three processes defined that you can use:

- Agile

- CMMI

- Scrum

Let us now take a look at these so you know their features and differences.

## Agile, CMMI, and Scrum

When you look at the templates you can see that they do not differ very much. The main difference is seen in the work item types they provide. We will soon look at these in more detail but simplified we can say that Scrum is the most lightweight and CMMI (Capability Maturity Model Integration) offers support for a more formal process where formal change management is important.

I will describe these now so that you can better evaluate which model is right for you and your organization.

## Scrum

The Scrum process is of course built upon the Scrum framework. Microsoft has worked with Scrum.org when they developed the Scrum process for TFS/VSTS and this is evident when you look at the terminology used in the process.

Figure 4-11 shows work items that work on three different levels. The Scrum process lets you manage work items at the portfolio level as well as the backlog level (work in sprints) as you can see in Figure 4-11 as well. You can see that you have Epics and Feature work items that will help you handle the portfolio backlog level. You can use TFS/VSTS to implement a program team that manages the overall high-level requirements using these two work item types. For the daily work in sprints, one or more teams can have a subset of the portfolio backlog that is dedicated to that specific team while other teams have their own subsets independent of the other teams. In Chapter 6, you will see how you can use the features of TFS/VSTS to set up such a scenario.

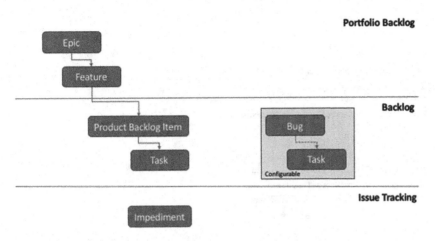

*Figure 4-11.* *The Scrum process and some of its work items*

Development teams usually work with work items on the backlog level. Here you find product backlog items (PBIs) and their associated tasks. You can also configure bugs and their tasks to be part of this level (see Figure 4-12). These work items are followed up only on remaining work, just like from the agile world.

*Figure 4-12.* *Working with bugs on the backlog level*

It is configurable how you work with bug (Figure 4-13). You can allow bugs to be seen on the boards and backlogs on the same level as requirements or tasks. Or you can choose not to have bugs appear on the boards and backlogs at all. You can change the desired behavior when you want so you are not locked in to the first choice you make.

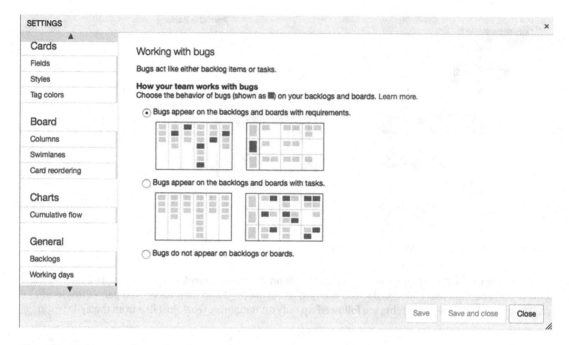

*Figure 4-13.* *You can change how bugs appear in the settings for backlogs and boards*

To manage issues that arise during a project, you can use impediments.

# Agile

The agile process has been developed in collaboration with the Agile alliance. Originally it was called Microsoft Solutions Framework (MSF) for agile, but now it is only referred to as the agile process in TFS/VSTS.

This process is aimed at supporting agile teams, even those that use Scrum as their process. It tracks development and test activities separately, just like the Scrum process. It also has three levels of work items as you saw in the Scrum process; see Figure 4-14.

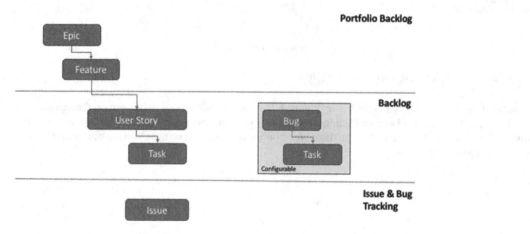

*Figure 4-14.* *The agile process in TFS/VSTS*

If you compare Figures 4-11 and 4-14, you can see that they are very similar. Only the names seem different. For instance, impediments for Scrum tracking are called *issues* in the agile process. Likewise, requirements are called user stories in the agile process and product backlog items in the Scrum process. The difference is more evident if you look at how the requirements are documented (see Figures 4-15 and 4-16).

***Figure 4-15.*** *The requirements work item in the Scrum process (called a product backlog item)*

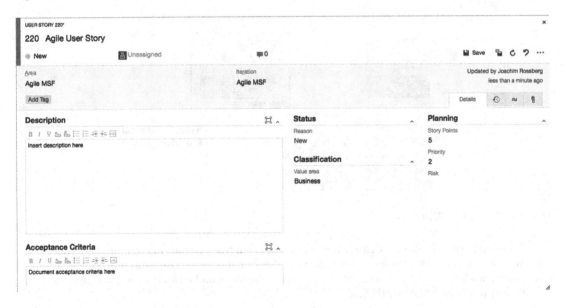

***Figure 4-16.*** *The requirements work item in the agile process (user story)*

Comparing these two figures, you can see that much is similar—like the Description and Acceptance criteria. But if you look at the details, you can find things that differ. The field for estimating a requirement is called Effort in the Scrum process and Story Points in the agile process.

Another difference is how you track your progress. In the agile process tasks support tracking Original Estimate, Remaining Work, and Completed Work and in the Scrum process you only track Remaining Work. In my view only remaining work is important but I do realize some organizations have demand for tracking more than this.

Take some time and study the different work item forms in your own environment so that you choose which method is best for your organization. But keep in mind that, as the next chapter will show, you can always customize the process.

## Capability Maturity Model Integration (CMMI)

The last process we will talk about is called CMMI. CMMI is a more formal project methodology and Wikipedia summarizes it like this: "Capability Maturity Model Integration (CMMI) is a process improvement training and appraisal program and service administered and marketed by Carnegie Mellon University (CMU) and required by many DoD and U.S. Government contracts, especially in software development. CMU claims CMMI can be used to guide process improvement across a project, division, or an entire organization. CMMI defines the following maturity levels for processes: Initial, Managed, and Defined. Currently supported is CMMI Version 1.3. CMMI is registered in the U.S. Patent and Trademark Office by CMU." See more at https://en.wikipedia.org/wiki/Capability_Maturity_Model_Integration.

The work item types in CMMI are also on three levels like the two former processes you looked at (Figure 4-17). In this process, requirements are in fact called *requirements* and not user stories or PBIs.

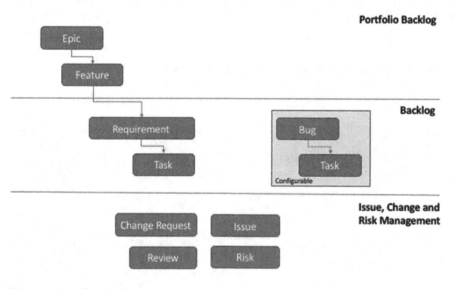

*Figure 4-17.* *The CMMI process*

Furthermore you can also see that you have more work item types for tracking your projects. You have work items for change requests, issues, reviews, and risk management. Using this process, you can implement a formal change-management process like the one found in, for instance, Information Technology Infrastructure Library (ITIL).

**ITIL**, formerly an acronym for Information Technology Infrastructure Library, is a set of practices for IT Service Management (ITSM) that focuses on aligning IT services with the needs of business. In its current form (known as ITIL 2011 edition), ITIL is published as a series of five core volumes, each of which covers a different ITSM lifecycle stage. Although ITIL underpins ISO/IEC 20000 (previously BS15000), the International Service Management Standard for IT service management, there are some differences between the ISO 20000 standard and the ITIL framework.

ITIL describes processes, procedures, tasks, and checklists that are not organization-specific, but can be applied by an organization for establishing integration with the organization's strategy, delivering value, and maintaining a minimum level of competency. It allows the organization to establish a baseline from which it can plan, implement, and measure. It is used to demonstrate compliance and to measure improvement (https://en.wikipedia.org/wiki/ITIL).

Figure 4-18 also shows differences between how requirements are documented in CMMI compared to the two other requirements types you have seen. You can quickly see that it is more details that can be filled out by default. And like the agile process, CMMI also supports tracking original estimate, remaining work, and completed work at the task level.

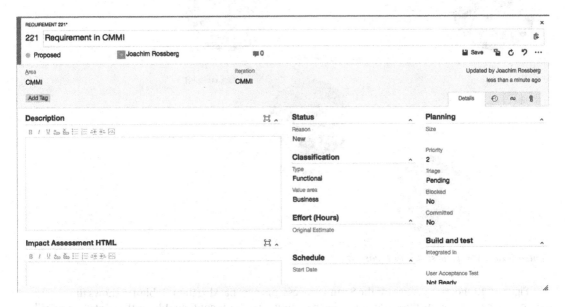

***Figure 4-18.*** *The requirements work item in the CMMI process (requirement)*

There are other work item types as well in these processes. These are the same for all processes. We will take a look at them shortly but first a few words on work item states.

## Workflow States

Workflow states support tracking the status of work as it moves from a new state to a closed or a done state. In TFS/VSTS a workflow consists of a set of states, the valid transitions between the states, and the reasons for transitioning the work item to the selected state (see Figure 4-19).

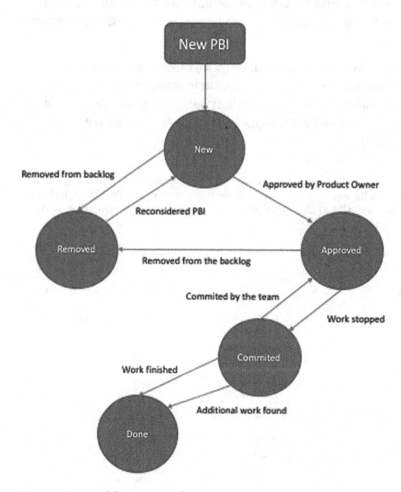

***Figure 4-19.*** *Workflow states and reasons*

Figure 4-19 shows the states for the Scrum process, product backlog item. Table 4-1 shows the differences in states for the three processes. Keep in mind that this is configurable, as the next chapter will show.

*Table 4-1.* *The Work Flow States for the Three Processes*

| Tracking Area | Scrum | Agile | CMMI |
|---|---|---|---|
| Workflow states | New | New | Proposed |
| | Approved | Active | Active |
| | Committed | Resolved | Resolved |
| | Done | Closed | Closed |
| | Removed | Removed | |

When you change the state of a work item to removed, closed, or done, the system behaves like this:

**Closed** or **done**: Closed or done work items do not appear on the portfolio backlog and backlog pages. However, they do appear on the sprint backlog pages, Kanban board, and task board. Also, when you change the portfolio backlog view to show backlog items (for example, to view Features to product backlog items), items in the closed and done states will appear.

**Removed**: Work items in this state do not appear on any backlog or board.

Work items are maintained in a team project as long as the team project is active. Even if you set them to closed, done, or removed, a record is kept in the data store, which means you can use them to create queries or reports.

If you need to permanently delete a work item, you can use the `witadmin destroywi` command-line tool. This tool is not discussed in this book.

Most work items that appear on backlogs and boards support any-to-any transitions. This means you can update the status of a work item using the Kanban board or the task board by dragging it to its corresponding state column.

You can also change the workflow so that you can have the states, transitions, and reasons that you need in your team or organization. More on this in the next chapter.

## Work Item Types For All Processes

There are some work item types that are the same for all three processes. They have three different purposes:

- Support Microsoft Test Manager (MTM)
- Support Feedback Request
- Support My Work and Code Review

Let's now briefly take a look at them.

## Work Items that Support MTM

Testers and test managers will often work with these work item types. The goal of this book is not to discuss testing in general, but we include a brief example here. Many test efforts are structured like this:

A *test plan* is created for a sprint using MTM or the web client. The test plan contains the high-level view of the testing effort. There is a Test Plan work item type included in all processes that you can use.

One or more *test suites* (another work item type) are created and included in the test plan. The suites themselves include one or more *test cases* (work item type). The test cases are used to describe step-by-step how a tester should test the application or functionality you are developing. Test cases are often associated with a requirement so that you can see which tests are covering a specific requirement.

So by using test plans, test suites, and test cases, you can structure your testing efforts in a way that gives you traceability and visibility into your tests (see Figure 4-20). You can generate reports and graphs that show the status of these work item types.

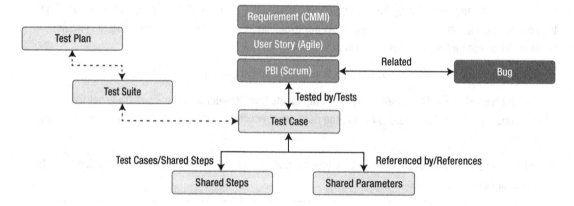

***Figure 4-20.*** *Workflow states and reasons*

There are two more work item types for testing, as you can see in Figure 4-20:

- *Shared steps*: These are test steps that you can reuse in many test cases. They can help you remove redundant test steps by allowing you to reuse them later.

- *Shared parameters*: When you write a manual test, you often want to specify that the test should be repeated several times with different test data. For example, if your users can add different quantities of a product to a shopping cart, you want to check that a quantity of 200 works just as well as a quantity of 1. To do this, you insert parameters in your test steps. Along with the test steps, you provide a table of parameter values. These parameters can be used to create shared parameters so that you can reuse them in other test cases as well.

When you develop your application you usually want stakeholders or end users to provide feedback on what you have done. Using the feedback functionality of TFS/VSTS, you can ask reviewers to provide videos, screenshots, type-written comments, and ratings. Their feedback is captured into work items that you can review and use to create a bug or suggest a new backlog item. There are two work item types you can use:

- Feedback request

- Feedback response

The last two work item types we will discuss are aimed at code reviews. Code reviews are a critical part of software development. They help you keep your defect count down as well as give you opportunity to learn from other people's code. A third benefit is that code reviews also allow teams to communicate changes to the application with their peers.

In TFS, you find two work items that help you with the code reviews:

- *Code review request*: This is a request a developer creates and sends to a peer asking for a review of some part of the code.

- *Code review response*: A response gets created when the code review request goes out and the reviewer can choose to accept or reject the review.

# Summary

This chapter has discussed many concepts regarding work items and processes in TFS and VSTS. You have seen how the work item tracking system works and how work items can help you increase both visibility and traceability. To put it simply, work items are the core of TFS/VSTS. Almost everything you do involves work items in one way or the other.

Which work items you have at your disposal is determined by the process you choose for your project. Out of the box you'll find three processes—Scrum, agile, and CMMI. These are similar in many ways but some things are different.

If a process is not sufficient for your needs, you can adjust it and add or remove things as you want. This is the focus of the next chapter.

■ ■ ■

# CHAPTER 5

# Customizing the Process Template in TFS

In the last chapter you could see that the process defines basically all aspects of your TFS/VSTS project. In the process, you get all definitions of which work items you can use and the information you collect for them. But sometimes you'll need to change the default process and perhaps add fields or change the work flow states. This chapter shows you the options you have.

## Process Customization

As you have seen so far in this book, it is essential to automate the ALM process to fully realize the benefits of it. TFS can quite you a lot by letting you have one or more process templates on the TFS server that define the way you work with the ALM process.

In this section, we'll take a look at how you can modify the TFS process templates in both TFS on-premise and Visual Studio Team Services.

The whole point of an extensible product such as TFS is that you can customize it to your needs. One of the biggest advantages of TFS is the capability to customize the process template so that you can realize your ALM process in the tools you use for your projects. Let's take a closer look at how the process template is built and how it can be changed by using the extensible features of TFS.

### Modifying the Process Template In TFS On-Premise

There are two ways to modify the XML files for the project templates. You can use manual customization or you can use the Process Editor, which is a power tool from Microsoft.

If you are daring, you can manually edit the XML files. This can be done by exporting the files from the TFS server using the `witadmin` command-line tool. See `https://msdn.microsoft.com/en-us/library/dd236914.aspx` for more information on that. Or you can use the Process Template Manager that comes with the TFS power tools.

© Joachim Rossberg 2016
J. Rossberg, *Agile Project Management using Team Foundation Server 2015*,
DOI 10.1007/978-1-4842-1870-9_5

You can update the work items (or the whole process) of an existing template (see Figure 5-1) or if you are even more daring, you can start from scratch. We suggest you modify an existing process template.

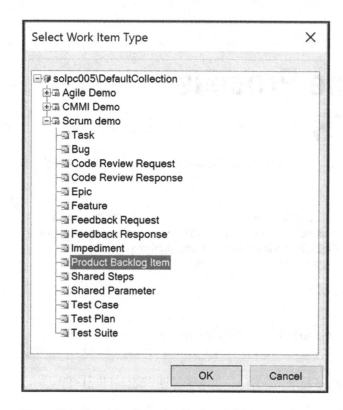

***Figure 5-1.*** *Exporting (downloading) a work item type from TFS by using the Process Template Manager*

Later in the chapter we will look at the possibilities of modifying the process template using VSTS.

After you have the work item in Visual Studio, you can start modifying all aspects of it. In Figure 5-2, you can see an excerpt of what one of the XML files looks like when seen in VS. Note the nice user interface you get with the Process Template Editor: You do not have to see the pure XML if you don't want to.

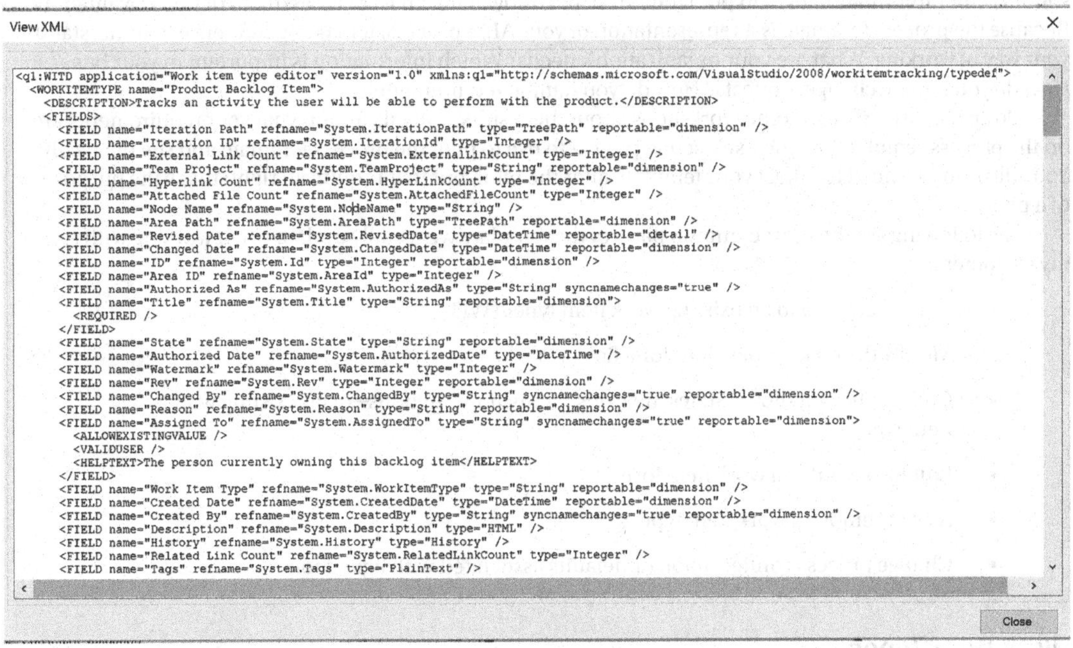

View XML

```xml
<q1:WITD application="Work item type editor" version="1.0" xmlns:q1="http://schemas.microsoft.com/VisualStudio/2008/workitemtracking/typedef">
  <WORKITEMTYPE name="Product Backlog Item">
    <DESCRIPTION>Tracks an activity the user will be able to perform with the product.</DESCRIPTION>
    <FIELDS>
      <FIELD name="Iteration Path" refname="System.IterationPath" type="TreePath" reportable="dimension" />
      <FIELD name="Iteration ID" refname="System.IterationId" type="Integer" />
      <FIELD name="External Link Count" refname="System.ExternalLinkCount" type="Integer" />
      <FIELD name="Team Project" refname="System.TeamProject" type="String" reportable="dimension" />
      <FIELD name="Hyperlink Count" refname="System.HyperLinkCount" type="Integer" />
      <FIELD name="Attached File Count" refname="System.AttachedFileCount" type="Integer" />
      <FIELD name="Node Name" refname="System.NodeName" type="String" />
      <FIELD name="Area Path" refname="System.AreaPath" type="TreePath" reportable="dimension" />
      <FIELD name="Revised Date" refname="System.RevisedDate" type="DateTime" reportable="detail" />
      <FIELD name="Changed Date" refname="System.ChangedDate" type="DateTime" reportable="dimension" />
      <FIELD name="ID" refname="System.Id" type="Integer" reportable="dimension" />
      <FIELD name="Area ID" refname="System.AreaId" type="Integer" />
      <FIELD name="Authorized As" refname="System.AuthorizedAs" type="String" syncnamechanges="true" />
      <FIELD name="Title" refname="System.Title" type="String" reportable="dimension">
        <REQUIRED />
      </FIELD>
      <FIELD name="State" refname="System.State" type="String" reportable="dimension" />
      <FIELD name="Authorized Date" refname="System.AuthorizedDate" type="DateTime" />
      <FIELD name="Watermark" refname="System.Watermark" type="Integer" />
      <FIELD name="Rev" refname="System.Rev" type="Integer" reportable="dimension" />
      <FIELD name="Changed By" refname="System.ChangedBy" type="String" syncnamechanges="true" reportable="dimension" />
      <FIELD name="Reason" refname="System.Reason" type="String" reportable="dimension" />
      <FIELD name="Assigned To" refname="System.AssignedTo" type="String" syncnamechanges="true" reportable="dimension">
        <ALLOWEXISTINGVALUE />
        <VALIDUSER />
        <HELPTEXT>The person currently owning this backlog item</HELPTEXT>
      </FIELD>
      <FIELD name="Work Item Type" refname="System.WorkItemType" type="String" reportable="dimension" />
      <FIELD name="Created Date" refname="System.CreatedDate" type="DateTime" reportable="dimension" />
      <FIELD name="Created By" refname="System.CreatedBy" type="String" syncnamechanges="true" reportable="dimension" />
      <FIELD name="Description" refname="System.Description" type="HTML" />
      <FIELD name="History" refname="System.History" type="History" />
      <FIELD name="Related Link Count" refname="System.RelatedLinkCount" type="Integer" />
      <FIELD name="Tags" refname="System.Tags" type="PlainText" />
```

Close

***Figure 5-2.*** *Example of a process template XML file in Visual Studio*

The Process Template Editor is a useful tool that Microsoft provides as an integrated part of the Team Foundation Server Power Tools for VSTS. You can find the power tools at this URL: `https://visualstudiogallery.msdn.microsoft.com/898a828a-af00-42c6-bbb2-530dc7b8f2e1`.

Team Foundation Server Power Tools installs Visual Studio Team System Process Editor, which is a process template editor for editing TFS process templates inside the Visual Studio IDE (see Figure 5-3).

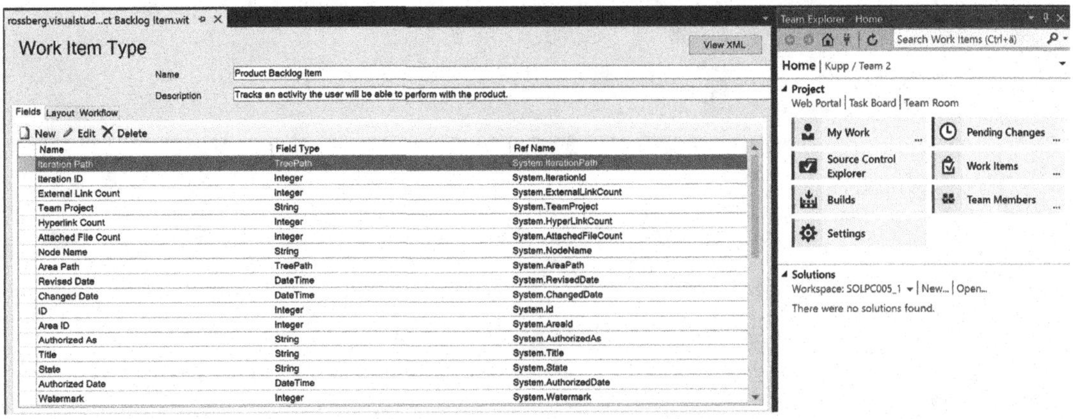


***Figure 5-3.*** *Editing the product backlog work item type from the Scrum process using the Process Editor inside Visual Studio*

## Common Adaptations of the Process Template

What are the most common things people change in the process template? I would say that this depends on your needs and I strongly suggest you consider your needs before starting to customize the templates. You should gather information to help point out these needs by doing an ALM assessment or other evaluation. Because the process template is a representation of your ALM process, it makes good sense to understand your way of working. What are your organization's needs? Which information is important in your bugs? How do you handle change requests? How do you handle requirements?

Do an assessment, run some workshops about the results, and talk about what your requirements are on the process template(s). Then select one project to use to pilot the process template and see the results. You will probably need to adjust your template after the pilot, but that is quite all right; that's the purpose of a pilot.

The following are the most common parts of the template we usually update when working with my customers.

- Add a new field to an existing work item types (WIT)

- Modify the pick list of values for a field

- Change the workflow—States, Reasons, Transitions, Actions—of an existing work item type

- Edit the layout of a work item form

- Add or remove a work item type

- Change process configuration or defaults associated with agile tools

## Work Item Types

You can use the work item types that Microsoft ships with VSTS in the three templates. But as mentioned earlier, we think you should really consider your own needs in the organization and make adjustments to these. Your organization might need more work items or might need to extend the information required for them. If your project managers use Microsoft Office Project, you might want to change the mapping between fields in TFS against fields in Project. Another thing to consider is the workflow of the work items. How is the process in your organization? Which states can a bug transition between? Microsoft supplies a set of default work item instances when a project is created. These represent tasks that need to be done in all projects. Your organization might have different needs for default work items.

## Work Item Queries

What information do you need to query about your work items? If you have made many changes to the work items, you might also need to change the queries so they reflect these changes. What queries does your ALM process need? In Figure 5-4, you can see the queries of the MSF for Scrum.

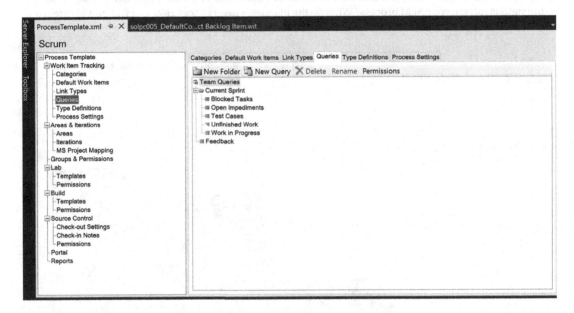

*Figure 5-4.* *The work item queries in the Scrum process*

## Reports

This is something that most of our customers have modified. The reports in the processes are very good. Figure 5-5 shows one of them, representing how much work is left in a project. In choosing which reports and information you need, we once again come back to the fact that this is something that you need to discuss with your project teams and also with stakeholders and managers. What information is important to the various roles in your ALM process? What do the managers need to see? How can you provide great feedback on project status to the team?

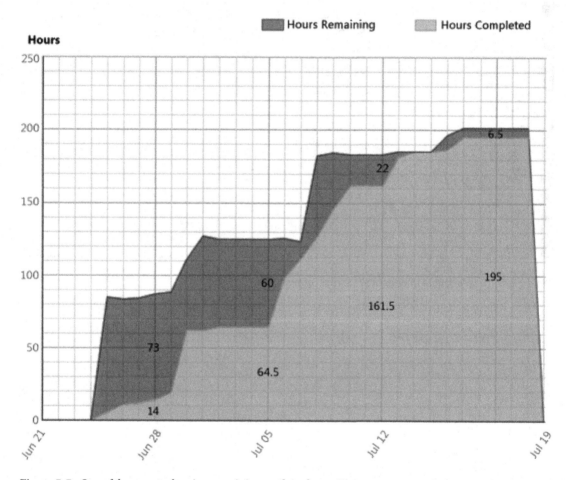

*Figure 5-5. One of the reports showing remaining work in the project*

## Areas and Iterations

Areas and iterations are interesting concepts. Iterations are just as they sound, basically. You use iterations to name the different versions of your project. You can name them anything you want. We have most often used the names Iteration 1, 2, 3, and so on, but that is up to you to decide. You can nest these and build an iteration hierarchy if you want.

Areas are labels you can attach to just about anything. One customer uses labels named after their windows or web forms in their projects. Another uses them for each component in their system. Then they can use areas and iterations to describe which areas (forms) belong to a certain iteration.

What we want to say about this is that you can use areas and iterations to label specific parts of your projects. These concepts are flexible, and you have the freedom to use them as you want. All work items can later be labeled with both an area and an iteration. Depending on your ALM process, you might use this for various reasons. If you run a project using RUP, you might want to use the iterations by naming them after the phases of RUP. Then you can nest iterations below each phase depending on your need. Figure 5-6 shows an example of what this could look like. And if during the project, you need more iterations in one phase, you can simply add them.

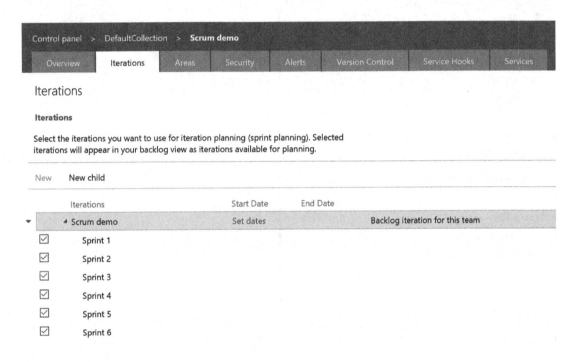

***Figure 5-6.*** *Areas and iterations in the team settings*

It is all up to you what you want to use these two categorizations for. In our opinion, they are very useful. They give you an enormous freedom in how you set up your projects, so we suggest you make good use of them.

## Modifying Work Items

Microsoft encourages you to modify your process template. One important thing we have found worth modifying are the work items. Many organizations we have seen have needed information in their work items that is not available in the three Microsoft templates. In those cases, we have adjusted the work items to better fit in the organization. This has turned out very successful in all cases. One thing we have changed is the workflow of the work items.

## How to Open the Process Template

You could start creating an entire new process template if you want, but it is far easier to start by modifying an existing one. First you need to download the process template from the TFS server. In Team Explorer, go to settings (see Figure 5-7) and choose Process Template Manager below Team Project Collection.

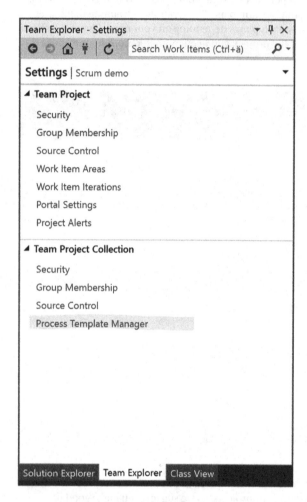

*Figure 5-7.* *Starting the Process Template Manager from Team Explorer*

Select a process template for downloading and click on Download in the Process Template Manager (Figure 5-8). Select a location to download the process template. Close the Process Template Manager when you are done.

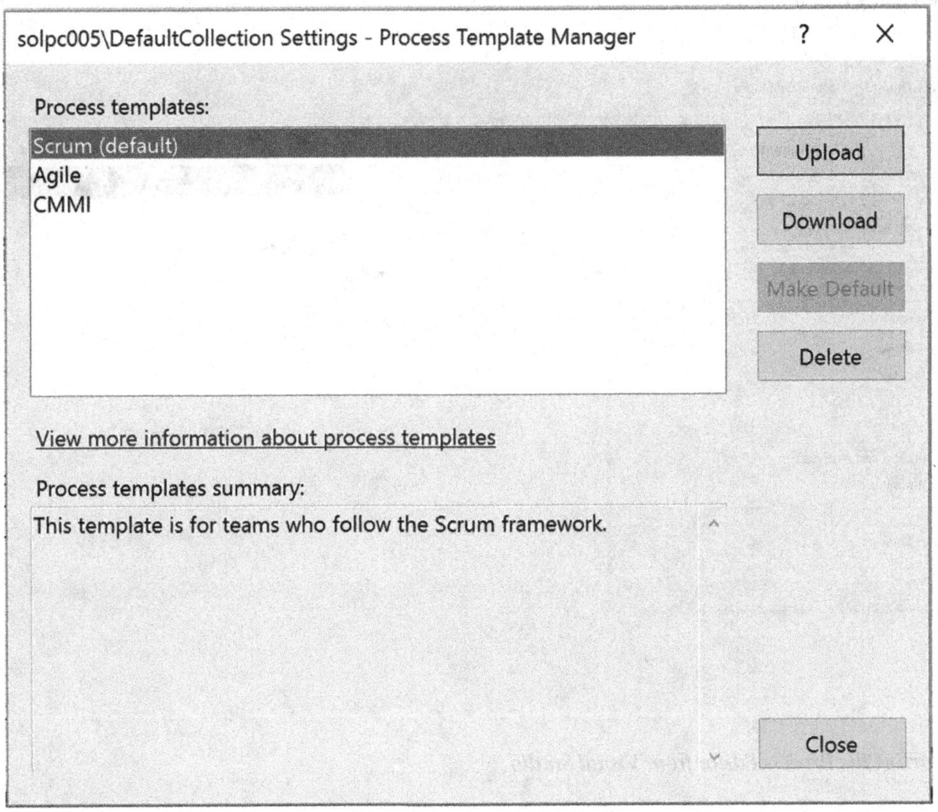

*Figure 5-8. Selecting a process to download*

To modify the process template you just downloaded, go to the Tools menu in Visual Studio and start the Process Template Editor (see Figure 5-9). You are provided with several options for what you can edit. As you see here, you can chose to edit the downloaded process template file(s) or select an item from the server. With the latter option, you edit the current installed process template, thereby changing all future projects created using that template.

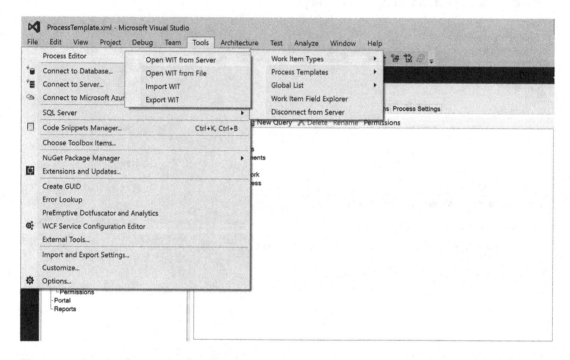

**Figure 5-9.** *Starting the Process Editor from Visual Studio*

Once you have finished editing a downloaded process template, you can rename it and upload it to the server as a new process template that becomes available for all new team projects.

## Work Item Fields

The default work items in TFS include a lot of information in their fields. But sometimes (quite often) we need to include more or maybe remove some fields so that the work items better fit our needs. You can do this by using the Process Template Editor. Figure 5-10 shows the fields from the product backlog item in the Microsoft Scrum template. You can see their names and what data type they are, and also the Ref Name.

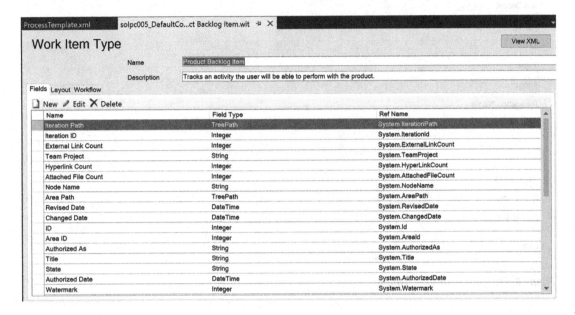

*Figure 5-10. The fields in the PBI WI from the Microsoft Scrum template*

If you double-click on a field, you are presented with the Field Definition as seen in Figure 5-11. From this window, you can change all aspects of the field.

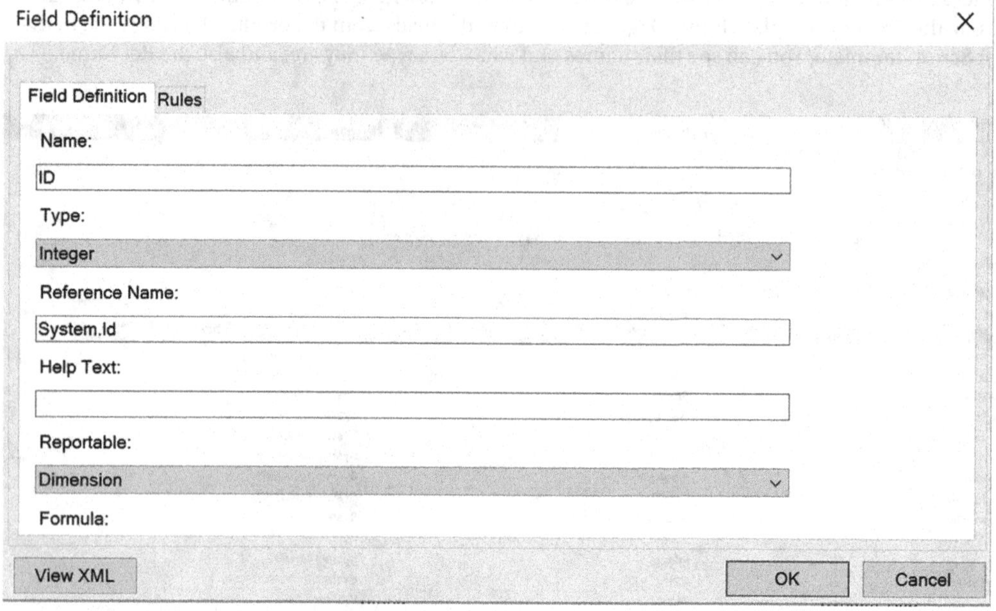

Field Definition                  ✕

Field Definition | Rules

Name:

ID

Type:

Integer     ⌄

Reference Name:

System.Id

Help Text:

Reportable:

Dimension     ⌄

Formula:

View XML             OK      Cancel

**Figure 5-11.** *Field Definition window*

There is a possibility to add different kinds of rules to the field, as you can see in Figure 5-12. So if you want to, you can control what values can be inserted into the field and a lot more.

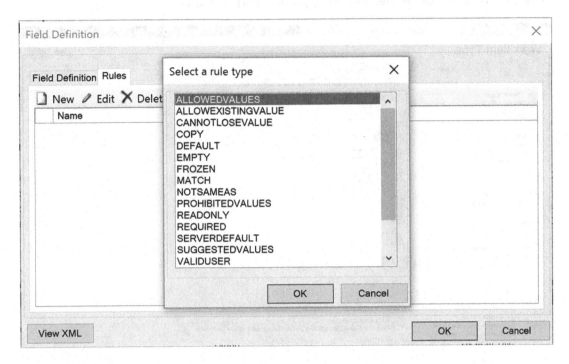

***Figure 5-12.*** *An example of a workflow for a bug work item*

To change the layout of the work item, you use the Layout tab (Figure 5-13). This might look a bit complex at first but once you start experimenting you will find that it is pretty easy to do a complete makeover if you want. Select Preview Form to see your changes (Figure 5-14).

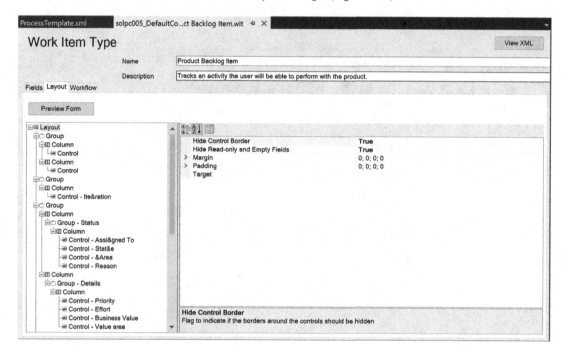

*Figure 5-13.* *The Layout tab for work items*

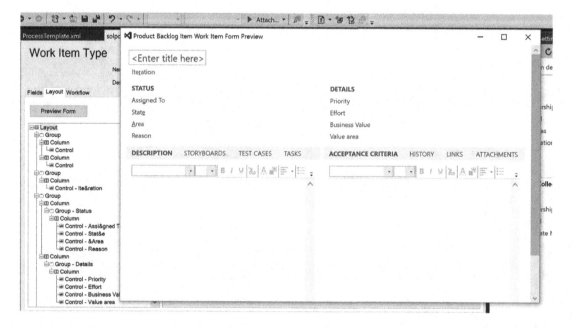

*Figure 5-14.* *Previewing the layout*

## Work Item Workflow

There is a workflow you can add to the work items. A bug work item has a State field, for instance, where the state flows through different levels. In this field, you can set the status of the bug. It can be active, closed, resolved, and so on. A typical workflow can look like Figure 5-15.

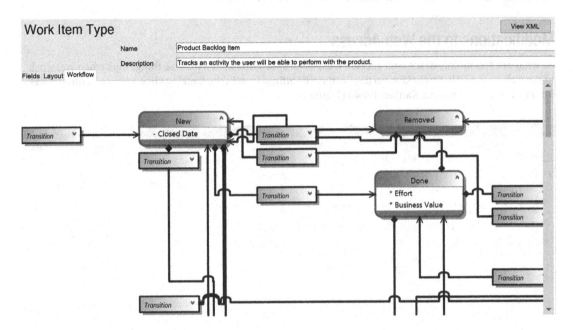

**Figure 5-15.** *An example of a workflow for a PBI work item*

In this example, you can see the workflow for a bug work item in Microsoft Scrum. This particular work item can have one of several states: New, Approved, Committed, Done, or Removed. The bug can transition through these states in the following ways:

- New to Approved
- New to Removed
- Approved to Committed
- Approved to Removed
- Committed to Done
- Removed to New

You can also let automatic transitions occur in the workflow. For example, if a closed bug is reopened because a new test shows there are still some errors in the code, you can automatically have the bug reassigned to the person who closed it. This way, you can save some work because you don't have to hunt down that person yourself.

## Modifying the Process Template in Visual Studio Team Services

Earlier it wasn't possible to modify the process template very much in Visual Studio Team Services (formerly Visual Studio Online). However, in the latest versions you can adjust quite a lot. There are also many ways you can configure the look and feel of the web access without modifying the process template. Let's take a look at this first, as this might be an adequate solution in many cases.

## Modifications to the Web Access

So what can you modify in the web access? Well, quite a lot associated with how things look when you work in the web-based GUI. By clicking on the Configure Settings icon in the backlog view, you reach the settings for how you can change the Kanban board (Figure 5-16).

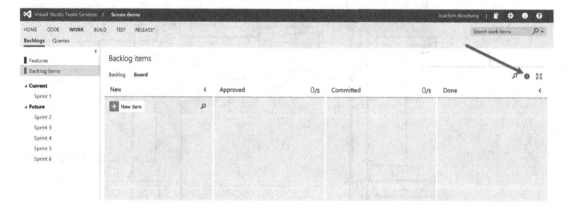

***Figure 5-16.*** *Configuring the Kanban board*

Doing this opens a new window (Figure 5-17) where you can modify the following aspects of the GUI:

- Cards
- Board
- Charts
- General

*Figure 5-17.* *Configuring the Kanban board*

You can change which fields you presents on the cards. Even though Microsoft has limited which fields you can show, you still have a fair collection at your disposal.

You can also create style rules that allows you to color-code a card based on a work item query. This way you can for instance determine that all bugs are colored red on the board (Figure 5-18).

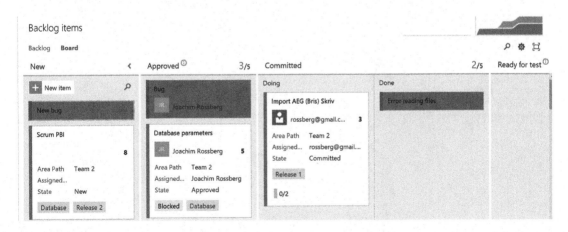

*Figure 5-18.* *Bugs are colored red using a style rule*

Should you have the need, you can also control that a specific tag is color-coded. Figure 5-19 shows that the tag Blocked is colored yellow and the tag Database is colored green. Both of these color codings will be of great use to you when you want to enhance visibility into your projects.

*Figure 5-19. You can color-code tags as well*

When it comes to *boards*, you can add and arrange columns on the board (Figure 5-20). If you are configuring the Kanban board, you can add a work in progress limit for instance. There is also an option to split a column into Doing and Done. This will create two columns of one so that you more easily can show that a specific PBI is ready for the next step in the process flow. In Figure 5-18, the Committed column is split using this method; this makes it visible to testers that a PBI is ready for test after developers are done working on the functionality. This is a good way to avoid adding a new column or state.

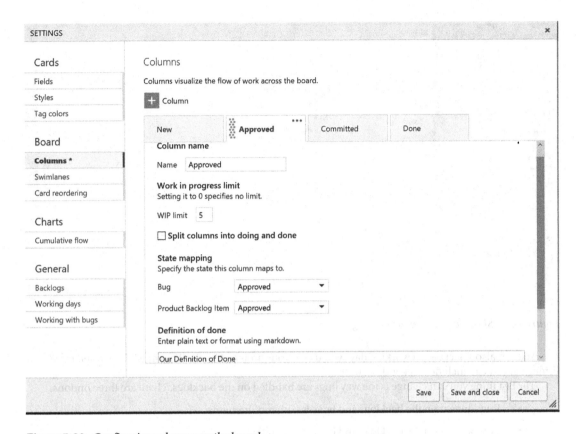

*Figure 5-20.* *Configuring columns on the board*

Another thing that you can do is add swimlanes to the board. For instance, in a project where I was working as a service manager for a large intranet we used swimlanes to keep track of different issues that came into the support group. Bugs had their own swimlane and change requests had their own as well. This way we could increase the visibility for all in the maintenance team as well as for stakeholders. Swimlanes are basically just a row in the board that you can use for whatever purpose you want. A nice inclusion by Microsoft.

Should you need to, you can also change the way work items are reordered on the board. You have two options:

- Work items reorder when changing columns, and the backlog reflects the new order

- Work items follow the backlog order when changing columns

The Charts section does not give you many options. You can basically just choose the time interval for the cumulative flow diagram. The default is 30 weeks but you can shorten that time span if you want.

Then we have one last section, which is the General section. From here you can select if you want to show epics, features, and backlog items on the backlog. In Figure 5-16, you can see that the backlog does not include epics, for instance. By selecting the Epics checkbox in Figure 5-21, you can tell VSTS to show epics as well.

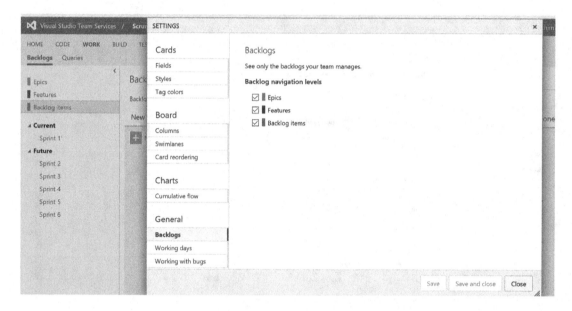

**Figure 5-21.** *Showing epics on the backlog*

You can also select which working days you use in your project. Most will obviously use Monday to Friday but you can include weekends as well.

The last thing you can change is the way bugs are handled on the backlogs. There are three options:

- Bugs appear on the backlogs and boards with requirements

- Bugs appear on the backlogs and boards with tasks

- Bugs do not appear on backlogs and boards

The choice is yours to make. Try which way works for your team; you can always evaluate and switch later.

## Modifications to the Process Templates in VSTS

In earlier versions of VSTS it wasn't possible to change many aspects of the process. You were stuck with what Microsoft had chosen for you. These days, however, you have many options to customize the process, which is a great step forward for VSTS.

There still are some differences between the ways you can modify the templates. VSTS for instance uses a different model than TFS for relating projects and process. In TFS, process templates are used as starting points for projects and once a project is created, the project is the scope you customize. In VSTS, on the other hand, a process is shared across multiple projects and that is the scope you customize.

Otherwise the syntax and structure used in defining the process is basically the same. There are only a few minor differences existing between templates you customize for import into VSTS and those you upload to support an on-premises TFS.

Let's take a look at how you access the process in template in VSTS. In Figure 5-22, you see that you should point at the configuration wheel in the top corner of the interface. When the configuration page is opened the first thing you need to do is to select the default collection in the top-left corner as seen in Figure 5-23.

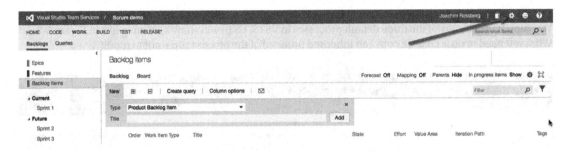

***Figure 5-22.*** *Accessing the configuration of the process in VSTS*

As you can see, these changes are made on all projects in the collection and not on a single project. In this figure, you can see that you have the three default processes from VSTS to work with.

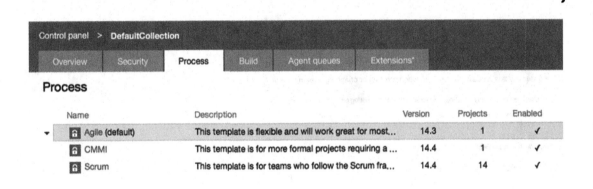

***Figure 5-23.*** *To see the processes in your VSTS instance, make sure you select the default collection*

To modify a process you click on the process name in the list. But here is one thing you need to consider. You cannot modify any of the three default processes in VSTS. VSTS will show a warning like in Figure 5-24. What you need to do is create a copy (an inherited process) of the process you want to modify.

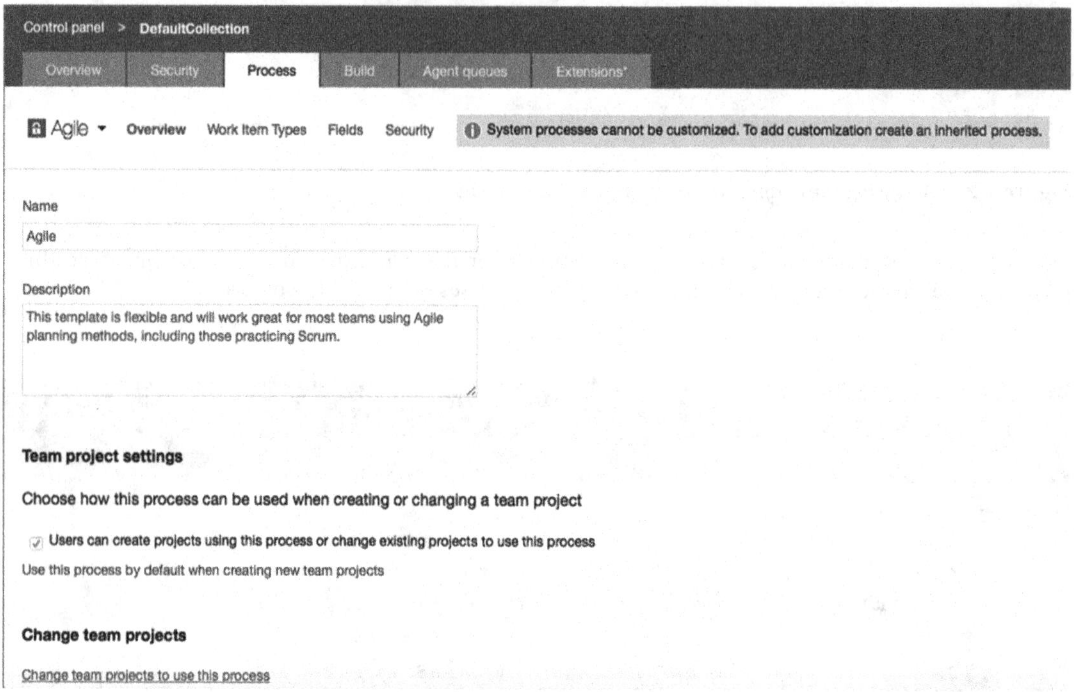

*Figure 5-24. You cannot modify any of the three system processes*

You do this by clicking on the link in the warning. This opens up a new window (Figure 5-25) where you can give the inherited process a name and a description. Once you are satisfied, you click Create Process.

*Figure 5-25.* *Creating a shared process for editing*

Now you can access the inherited process and start your editing. The first thing you see when you enter edit mode is the overview of your new process (called My Own Custom Agile in Figure 5-26). As you see, you can change the name of the process as well as the description. If you look closely you can also see that you can check a checkbox that allows you to create new projects based on the inherited process and also allow users to change existing projects to use this process. This is a very nice feature in some cases.

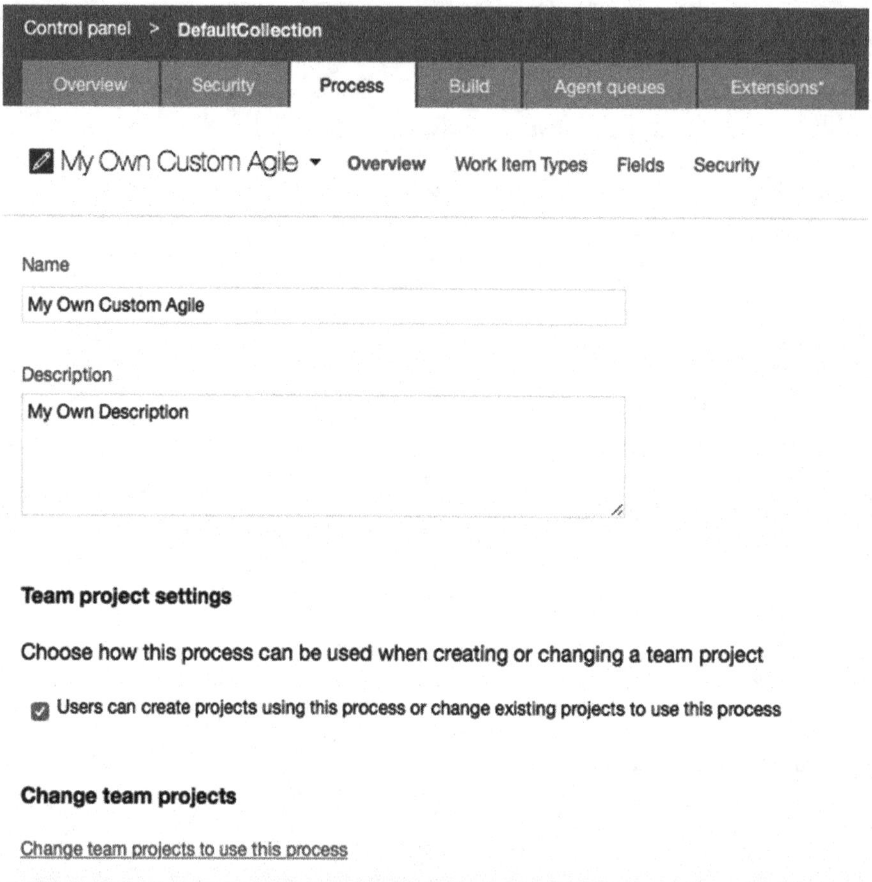

*Figure 5-26.* *Starting editing the inherited process*

What can you change while in editing mode? If you look at the Work Item Types tab (Figure 5-27), all work item types defined for the chosen process are visible on the left side of the page. For each type, you can change the following:

- Overview
- Layout
- Fields

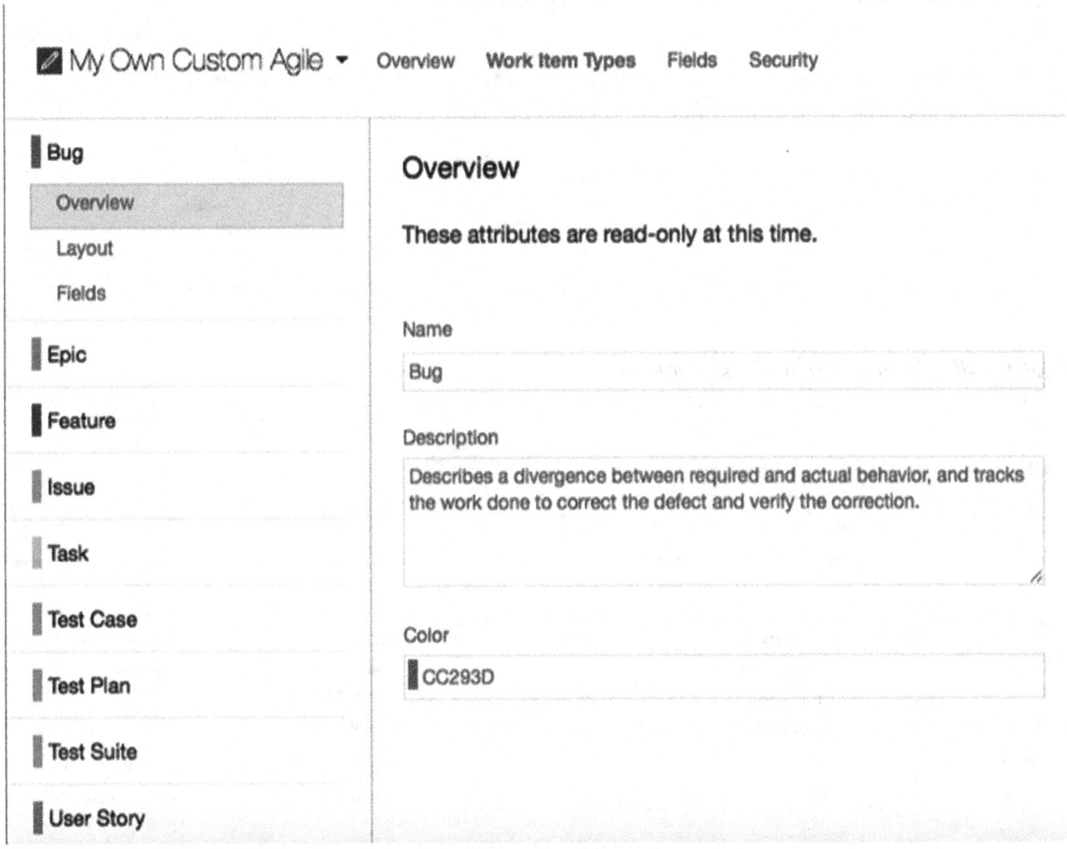

*Figure 5-27.* *Attributes in the overview view is read-only at this time*

The overview shows the name of the work item type as well as the color coding the work item type has. In Figure 5-27, you see the bug work item type and the fact that it will be displayed with a red color coding. At the time of writing it is not possible to change any of the information here but I suspect Microsoft will add this possibility later on.

Moving on to the layout. Figure 5-28 shows what the layout of a bug in the agile process looks like when you create a new bug. Look closely at the fields in the figure and compare them to the fields you can see in editing mode in Figure 5-29.

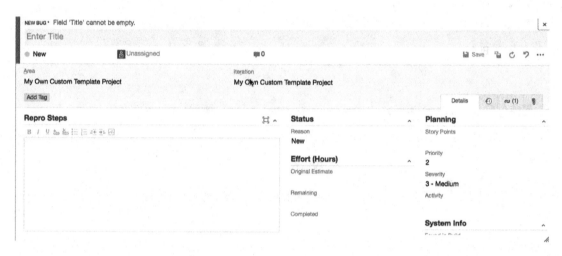

*Figure 5-28.* *The bug form in the agile process*

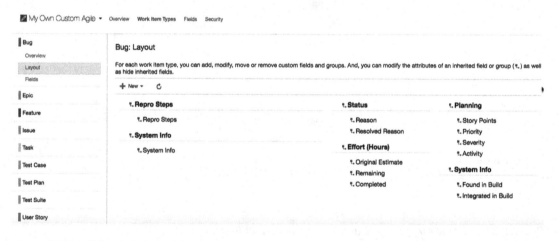

*Figure 5-29.* *Editing the bug work item type*

You can edit the bug to include more groups (Status is one group and Planning is another for instance) and add more fields below each group. The groups can be placed in two columns of the three columns of groups that Microsoft provides, as Figure 5-30 shows. You cannot place a new group in the first column.

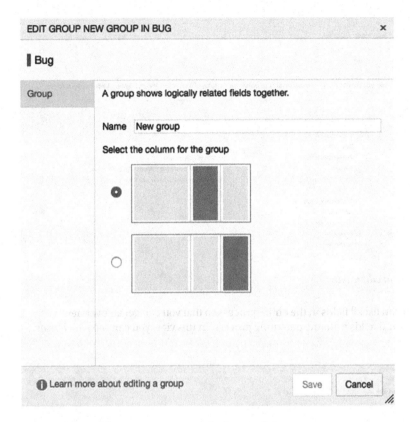

*Figure 5-30.* *Adding a new group on the bug work item type*

For each group, you can add, edit, or remove fields so that you can enter the information that your organization thinks is important for a work item type.

The fields view will let you add or modify the attributes of a custom field or the attributes of an inherited field (Figure 5-31). Keep in mind that you cannot modify system fields. In this view, you only work with the fields that are present in the work item type you are currently editing.

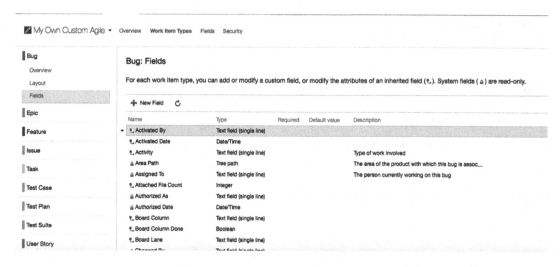

***Figure 5-31.*** *Working with fields in edit mode*

Figure 5-32 shows that you can list all fields in the entire process so that you can get an overview of them, including system fields and fields from the parenting process. In this view you can see which user story uses a specific field.

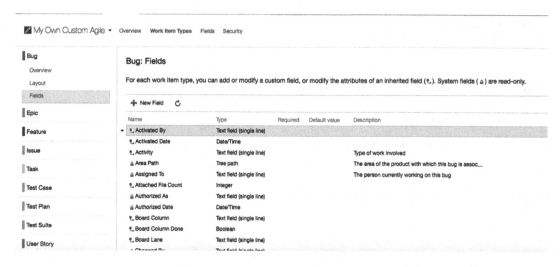

***Figure 5-32.*** *You can list all process fields and see which work item type includes the field*

You can also see that you have a security tab that you can use. In this view, you can select which TFS users are allowed to create or modify the processes in your VSTS instance.

Once you are done editing your process, you can access it and create a new VSTS project using your own customized process, as shown in Figure 5-33.

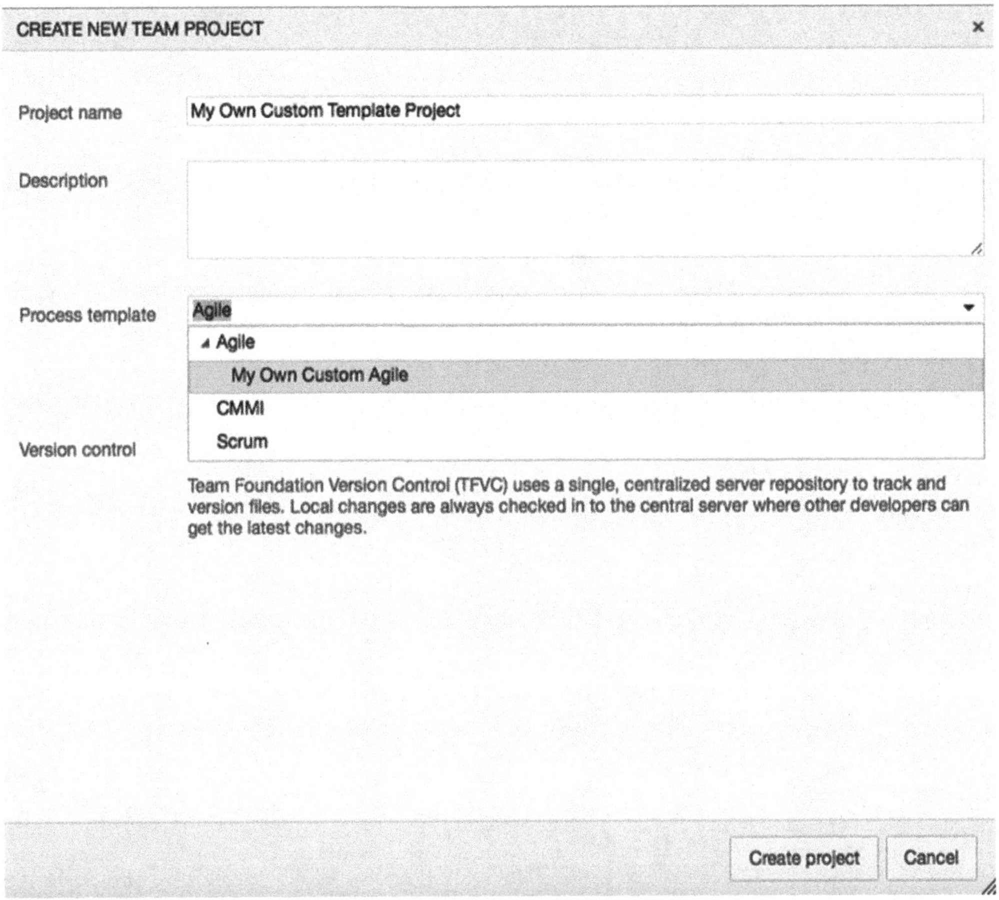

*Figure 5-33. After you have created a custom process, you can use it to create a new VSTS project*

# Summary

This chapter looked at how you can customize your process in TFS on-premise as well as in VSTS. Most customizations can be done on-premise but Microsoft has added great support for editing a cloud-based TFS project as well.

We will now move on to a short overview of how you can implement Extreme Programming (XP) practices into your TFS/VSTS projects. Many XP practices will increase code quality greatly and can be used even if you are running an un-agile project.

# CHAPTER 6

■ ■ ■

# Agile Practices in TFS

This chapter focuses on the more technical aspects of agile practices. They might not be directly linked to project management or product management but they are great ways to enhance the quality of your coding efforts. In Chapter 3, you saw a brief overview of Extreme Programming or XP as it is generally referred to. As you probably remember, you could see that as Scrum for instance does not say how you should work using this Scrum framework, XP is much more practice-oriented, giving you hands-on advice on how you should work.

XP focuses on 12 practices but some of them (regarding project management) overlap with what is covered by Scrum and in my opinion Scrum handles these better than XP. If I have a choice, I generally use Scrum as project management framework and XP for development tasks. This chapter focuses on the following practices from XP.

- Agile testing

- Test-driven development and automated testing

- Continuous integration and continuous delivery

- Coding standards

- Pair programming/peer-review

- Refactoring

Why do I focus on only these you might ask? Well because they, just as I wrote, are code quality enhancing. And also because they are very common for developers to use in agile projects. If you as a PO should understand all aspects of the definition of *done* (DoD), it is also important to understand topics that might come up in discussion regarding the DoD with the developers. Let's start with agile testing and move on from there.

## Agile Testing

Agile projects can often be challenging. You need to have the mindset that change will come and embrace that change. By working iteratively and delivering incrementally, you have a better chance of delivering what the customer wants, not what they thought they wanted several months earlier.

Delivering software incrementally at short intervals means that you need to rethink the testing approach you use. Working with incremental development typically means you need to do lots of regression testing to make sure the features you have developed and tested still continue to work as the product evolves. You need to have an efficient test process or else you will spend lots of time in the cycle preparing for testing rather than actually running the tests.

© Joachim Rossberg 2016
J. Rossberg, *Agile Project Management using Team Foundation Server 2015*,
DOI 10.1007/978-1-4842-1870-9_6

Take Amazon.com for instance. I have read many times that they deploy to production every 11.6 seconds (here is one reference: http://joshuaseiden.com/blog/2013/12/amazon-deploys-to-production-every-11-6-seconds/). Without knowing the actual process that Amazon.com uses to accomplish this, I can only guess that they have a lot of automated testing in place in order to make sure that new code does not interfere with old code.

To solve the problems and challenges, this implies you need to carefully design your tests. You need to maintain only the tests that give value to your product. As the product evolves through increments, so should the tests. You can choose to add only relevant tests to your regression test suite. To make the testing more efficient, you should automate the tests and include them in your continuous integration/continuous delivery workflow to get the most value from them.

# Acceptance Criteria

A wise man named Mathias Olausson (my boss and co-writer from time to time) once wrote, "Acceptance criteria are to testing what user stories are to product owners. Acceptance criteria sharpen the definition of a user story or requirement. We can use acceptance criteria to define what needs to be fulfilled for a product owner to approve a user story." This is very true indeed.

Chapter 3 covered some agile processes. One way to describe requirements is using user stories. When writing user stories, we usually write them like this:

- As a service repair I want to be able to view ticket details from the dashboard so that the tickets are easy to access when we're at our customers.

This is of course not the entire requirement, but just a description of it. You can detail a user story in different ways:

- Breaking down the story into several new stories

- Adding acceptance criteria

When discussing this story with the product owner, you could come up with questions such as these:

- How should the service rep view the tickets? Search? Filter?

- In what way will the service rep access the tickets? Over the web? Phone? Tablet?

- Is the ticket read-only or can the service rep edit it? Assign to someone else?

You then use this information to formulate acceptance criteria. Take for instance the question, "How should the service rep view the tickets?" From this, you could formulate acceptance criteria such as the following:

- A service rep should:

    - Be able to click the service ticket number in the list on the dashboard and see the details.

    - Be able to search by customer, geography, and time.

    - Be able to filter the results to get a better overview.

Hopefully this discussion will lead to more questions for the PO which helps you better understand what you should test. It will also help you define the product more clearly.

In TFS or VSTS, you can collect all this important information in a product backlog item (or user story or requirement depending on what process template you use).

The PBI gives good traceability to follow the requirement to its acceptance criteria. Figure 6-1 shows an example of how the Visual Studio Scrum template in VSTS shows this information.

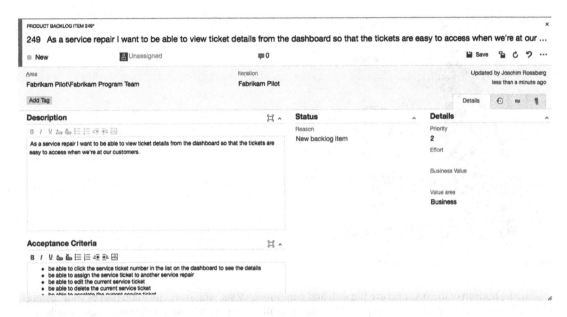

*Figure 6-1.* *Documenting acceptance criteria as part of a PBI*

# Evolving Tests

In an agile process where development is done in small increments, you also need to make sure that the tests follow this iterative way of working. The tests need to follow the flow of the application development; otherwise, you might have many problems along the line.

Early on you'll know very little about a new feature and typically need to run tests against all acceptance criteria defined for the requirement. When a feature has been completed, you should be confident it has been tested according to the test cases and that it works as expected. After that you only need to run tests to validate changes in the requirement. This means that you must have a process for how you know which tests to run.

However, running all tests manually will be tedious and take a lot of effort. Instead, you need to rethink how you design test cases. You could for instance think of your test base as a pyramid. Figure 6-2 shows how different types of tests can be put in proportion in this specific case.

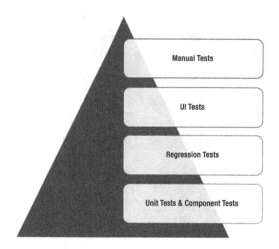

***Figure 6-2.*** *Proportions of types of tests*

At the bottom of the pyramid are the unit and component tests, which are the main part of your testing efforts. These tests are relatively cheap to create and maintain. But in order to test the system as a whole, you'll probably need to add regression tests that run end-to-end tests as well.

Some of the regression tests should be implemented as user interface tests to really how an end user would use the system. However, UI tests are more complex to design and maintain and it is often not practical to have more than a small set of these tests. Most of these tests can and should be automated to give you an efficient way to keep up with the changes in the product.

Using this way of designing your tests, you can see that you'll end up with a small amount of manual tests at the top of the pyramid. This means that manual tests will always be necessary to some extent.

The next section discusses a little about how TFS can help you manage your tests.

## Clients for Managing Tests

There are two options for managing tests in TFS 2015:

- Microsoft Test Manager, which is a desktop application
- Microsoft Web Test Case Manager, which is a web-based application

## Microsoft Test Manager

The Microsoft Test Manager, MTM, is a standalone desktop application and was included in the Visual Studio family when TFS 2010 was released. Microsoft Test Manager can be seen as the Visual Studio for testers, the one-stop shop for the entire test process. A tester can do almost all the testing activities within a single application.

At a high level, Microsoft Test Manager provides functionality for:

- *Exploratory testing using Microsoft Test Manager:* Record your actions while you perform a test without pre-planned steps.

- *Plan manual tests with Microsoft Test Manager:* Plan tests with the option of creating steps from recorded actions.

- *Run manual tests with Microsoft Test Manager:* Display the test case at the side of the screen while you perform the test. Automatically record your actions, screenshots, and other diagnostic data for inclusion in test results and bug reports.

- *Test configurations: specifying test platforms:* Create multiple versions of a test, to be performed on different hardware or software configurations.

- *Collect more diagnostic data in manual tests:* Collect event logs, IntelliTrace data, video, and other diagnostic data while you perform a test.

- *Testing Windows Store apps:* Collect diagnostic data and screenshots while you perform tests on a Windows 8 device or PC, with Microsoft Test Manager running on a separate PC.

- *Copying and cloning test suites and test cases:* Copy test suites or plans from one project to another.

- *Record and play back manual tests:* Record your keystrokes and gestures while you perform a test, and then repeat the actions rapidly on a later occasion.

- *Plan application tests from a Microsoft Excel or Microsoft Word document:* Use Microsoft Excel to edit test plans in bulk, and synchronize with plans embedded in Microsoft Word documents.

- *Test on a lab environment:* Gather diagnostic data from servers while you perform a test. Manage the assignment of server machines to testers. Quickly set up fresh test configurations by using virtual machines.

- *Tracking software quality:* Monitor the progress of your project by tracking the tests that pass or fail. Manage bugs.

- *Automate system tests:* Link test methods in code to emulate your manual tests so that they can be repeated regularly. Automate the deployment of your application and tests to a lab environment. Set up a completely automatic build-deploy-test workflow. Add existing automated tests from Visual Studio to your test suites.

Microsoft Test Manager comes with Visual Studio 2015 ALM Enterprise or Microsoft Test Professional 2015.

## Microsoft Web Test Case Manager

The second client for working with test cases is the Microsoft Web Test Case Manager, WTM, or the Test Hub. This is a fairly new addition to the Team Web Access, introduced with the TFS 2012 Update 2 release. WTM is a lightweight solution where you want the integrated testing experience with TFS but don't want to (or maybe cannot) install the MTM client.

As a core part of Team Foundation Server, the Test Hub enables you to create and run manual tests through an easy-to-use web-based interface that can be accessed via all major browsers on any platform.

The Test Hub isn't just for manual testers. It's a tool that product owners and business analysts can use to evaluate how their features measure up against the acceptance criteria. You can use it to keep track of acceptance criteria for requirements, and can later be used for sign-off. In summary, the Test Hub offers:

- Customization of workflows with test plan, test suite, and test case work items.

- End-to-end traceability from requirements to test cases and bugs with requirement-based test suites.

- Criteria-based test selection with query-based test suites.

- Excel-like interface with a grid for easy test case creation.

- Reusable test steps and test data with shared steps and shared parameters.

- Sharable test plans, test suites, and test cases for reviewing with stakeholders.

- Browser-based test execution on any platform.

- Real-time charts for tracking test activity.

To use the Microsoft Web Test Case Manager, you need to have a valid license for Microsoft Test Manager.

# Test-Driven Development

Test-Driven Development (TDD) is a practice originating from Kent Beck who is credited with having developed or "rediscovered" the technique. TDD is one of the core practices in Extreme Programming but has created lots of general interest in its own right. So even if you do not practice XP, you can still uses this practice as a way to help developers write better code.

TDD relies on the repetition of a very short development cycle: first developers write an (initially failing) automated test case that defines a desired improvement or new function, then they produce the minimum amount of code to pass that test, and finally they refactor the new code to acceptable standards. Kent Beck stated in 2003 that TDD encourages simple designs and inspires confidence.

Instead of designing a module, then coding it and then testing it, you turn the process around and do the testing first. To put it another way, you don't write a single line of production code until you have a test that fails.

In traditional software development, tests were thought to verify that an existing bit of code was written correctly. When you do TDD, however, your tests are used to define the behavior of a class before you write it.

---

■ **Note**   Using TDD, you'll want to run your tests frequently to get continuous feedback about the code. A change in code that breaks one or more tests is something you should become aware of immediately. You can configure Visual Studio 2015 to automatically run unit tests after a build so that as soon as you compile the code, you will also run all tests and get feedback on their result. This means that the feedback loop will be very short. This loop is the time (in this case) between developers making code changes and them getting feedback on whether the change was successful.

---

Earlier, the chapter looked at the test process in general and how it can be designed to support agile teams and agile testing. Initially, you should probably define and run your tests manually by using Microsoft Test Manager. After that you can choose which tests to automate; that subject is covered briefly next.

Automated tests can also be used to test non-functional requirements. You can continue to build on the same automated tests and create performance and load test sessions to validate production-like use of the system you are developing.

# Working with Automated Tests

In order to achieve the goals of automated testing, you need to plan ahead and think about what you really want to get out of your automation efforts. Visual Studio 2015 will help you set up your test environment and select which test types to use.

Visual Studio 2015 has support for a number of different test types ranging from basic unit tests to automated UI tests up to complete load-testing capabilities (see Table 6-1). What is really nice when working with tests in Visual Studio is its shared tooling for designing and running tests. This is very convenient because you can start by learning the type of test you want to begin working with and then leverage the framework and determine how you design, run, and follow up test runs. As you add types of automated tests, you do not have to learn new practices. You just add the new ones to the existing platform.

***Table 6-1.*** *Description of Test Types Supported in Visual Studio 2015*

| Test Types | Purpose |
| --- | --- |
| Basic Unit Test | An empty unit test. |
| Unit Test | A basic unit test with a TestContext and additional test attributes. |
| Coded UI Test | A coded UI test. |
| Coded UI Test Map | Creates a UI test map that can be used to split the UI definitions in a coded UI test into smaller pieces. |
| Generic Test | Can wrap an existing function into an MSTest. |
| Ordered Test | Can be used to control how a set of tests are executed. |
| Web Performance Test | Records a web test using Internet Explorer. |
| Load Test | Launches a wizard to generate a load test configuration. |

Table 6-1 explains the purpose of some test types in Visual Studio.

The following sections on continuous integration and continuous delivery are inspired by my boss, Mathias Olausson. He is an expert in this area, so make sure to check out his recent book about continuous delivery with Visual Studio ALM 2015 at `http://www.apress.com/9781484212738?gtmf=s`. It is a great reference on this topic.

# Continuous Integration

*"Continuous integration is a software development practice where members of a team integrate their work frequently—usually each person integrates at least daily—leading to multiple integrations per day."*

—Martin Fowler

Continuous integration (CI) is a practice in XP that has come to be the de facto standard in agile projects. Martin Fowler was the person who introduced it to the more general public, but it was first named and proposed by Grady Booch in 1991 (`https://en.wikipedia.org/wiki/Grady_Booch`). CI is a practice that has the intention of integrating the codebase frequently. In combination with running automated unit tests in the developer's local environment and verifying they all passed before committing to the mainline, CI aims to make sure that the developer is not checking in code that breaks any other developer's code.

Over time this has evolved and now builds run on build servers, which automatically run the unit tests periodically or even after every commit and report the results to the developers. CI has spread outside the agile community and is now used frequently in other types of projects as well.

In addition to running the unit and integration tests, you can also run static and dynamic tests, measure and profile performance, extract and format documentation from the source code, and facilitate manual QA processes. This way, you get continuous quality control of your software as well.

An agile project requires new ways of working and, just like Scrum, aims to be all about common sense. But there are several problems with agile development from a deployment perspective, such as

- *Testing*: Since you develop your software incrementally in short iterations, you need to rethink how you test as well.

- *Cross-functional teams*: Ideally the team should be self-organized, meaning more people need to be able to deploy software.

- *Shippable product in every iteration*: In short iterations (perhaps a two-week sprint), it is no longer possible to spend a week on installation. Hence, you need to automate tasks that where previously manual.

Continuous integration can help resolve these issues. In fact, Scrum has a solution for this; use the retrospective to find ways to improve.

## Why Continuous Integration?

What will CI help you with then? Well, continuous integration will

- Reduce risks

- Reduce manual routines

- Create shippable software

- Improve confidence in the product

- Identify deficiencies early

- Reduce time

- Improve project visibility

Keep in mind that CI is not free of costs. You need to maintain your CI solution including the build environment over time. It can also take quite some effort to introduce into your organization. And don't forget that CI introduces costs for setting up the new build and infrastructure as well.

To get continuous integration working, the team needs to agree on some rules around the process. If the rules are not followed there is a potential risk that the quality of the result will degrade and people will lose confidence in the process. Mathias Olausson recommends using at least the following rules as a starting point:

- *Check in often*: The CI process needs changes to work. The smaller the changes you can commit and the more specific the changes are, the quicker you can react to things that go wrong.

- *Do not check in broken code*: Checking in often is great but don't overdo it. Don't check in code until it works and never check in broken code. If you need to switch context, use the "suspend" feature in TFS to put things aside for a while.

- *Fix broken builds immediately*: If you happen to break something, it is your responsibility to fix it.

- *Write unit tests*: The system needs to know what works and what does not. Unit tests and other inspection tools should be used to make sure the code does more than just compile.

- *All tests and inspections must pass*: With inspections in place you must pay attention to the result. Use feedback mechanisms to make people aware when something is broken.

- *Run private builds*: If you can do a test build before checking in, you can avoid committing things that don't work. TFS can build from a shelveset using a feature called Gated Checkin.

- *Avoid getting broken code*: Finally, if the build is broken don't get the latest code. Why go through the problem to work on code that doesn't work? Instead, use the version control system and get the latest version that worked.

Figure 6-3 shows a process that can be considered a complete CI solution and should be what you strive to achieve.

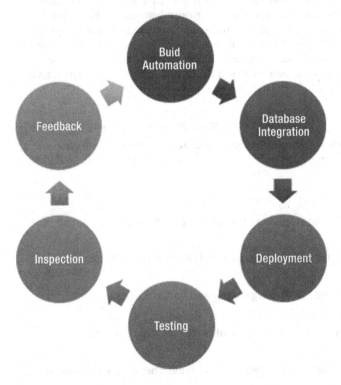

***Figure 6-3.*** *Components in the continuous integration process*

# Continuous Delivery

The problem with continuous integration is *not* that is is not a good solution. It's just that it can be a solution to a non-existing problem. Deployment as part of the CI flow is not just about automating the build, test, and release processes. You need to think about delivery to really add value to the deployment process.

Continuous integration is great and it gives you a framework for efficiently producing software in a controlled fashion. But to get the most out of it, you need to look at how it fits into the overall process of delivering software. In an agile project, you want to deliver working software in every iteration. Unfortunately, this is easier said than done; it often turns out that even if you implement CI and get the build process to produce a new installation package in a few minutes, it takes several days to get a new piece of software tested and released into production. So how can you make this work better?

Let's start by asking the following simple question:

*How long does it take to release one changed line of code into production?*

Probably the answer is much longer than you would want to. Why is this? First you must know more about how you release your product. Mathias Olausson says that even in organizations that follow good engineering practices, the release process is many times neglected. A common reason why this happens is simply because releasing software needs collaboration across different disciplines in the process. To improve the situation, you need to sit down with your team and document the steps required to go from a code change to the software released into production. Figure 6-4 shows a typical delivery process and in practice work happens sequentially as it's shown.

**Figure 6-4.** *A typical delivery process*

When you have come this far, you know a lot more about the delivery process, which means you can start optimizing the process.

1. Look at the steps in the process that take the most time and see what can be done to shorten them.

2. Look at the steps in the process that most often go wrong and understand what is causing this.

3. Look at the sequence of the steps and think about whether they need to be run in sequence.

Having looked at the process and asked the questions, you can now build a better process, as shown in Figure 6-5.

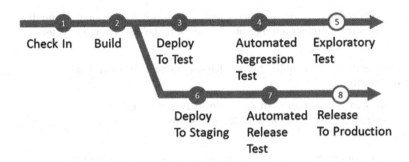

**Figure 6-5.** *An optimized delivery process*

In this model, the process is changed so that most of the steps are automated by implementing automated tests as well as automated build and deployment. Releasing to production automatically is not for the faint-hearted, so this would be done manually but using the same automated scripts as the automated deploy to test and staging environments. We do believe it's possible to automate even release to production, especially if you have had this working from the first iteration of the project. By doing so, you can build up confidence for the process and having seen it work throughout the development cycle should make you trust the process even in this critical stage. We have also parallelized the acceptance test and preparation of the production environment. By doing this in parallel, you can push the release to production as soon as the acceptance tests are green instead of the traditional stage to production first after the acceptance tests have passed.

Continuous delivery gives you a great practice to produce updates in a controlled and effective manner. But without an intentional release management discipline, it can lose much of its value. What you need to add to the picture is how the release planning ties into the deployment process and ensure that you know what features you want to deploy, where and when. This is not covered in the scope of this book, but refer to Mathias Olausson's book for more details and best practices.

# Coding Standard

A coding standard is an agreed upon set of rules that the entire development team uses throughout the project. The standard specifies a consistent style and format for source code, within the chosen programming language, as well as various programming constructs and patterns that should be avoided in order to reduce the probability of defects. The coding standard may be standard conventions specified by the language vendor (e.g., "The Code Conventions for the Java Programming Language" recommended by Sun), or defined by the development team.

Extreme Programming backers advocate code that is self-documenting to the furthest degree possible. This reduces the need for code comments, which can get out of sync with the code. This can be especially useful if you have a new developer coming in to write code or if you use many consultants. It will be easier to make sure that all developers adhere to the same coding standards so that the code will be maintainable over time.

In Visual Studio you can require that code analysis be run on all code projects in a team project by using the code analysis check-in policy. Requiring code analysis can improve the quality of the code that is checked into the code base. The feedback loop will be very short before the developers find any coding that is not following the standard.

Code analysis check-in policies are set in the team project settings and apply to each code project in the team project. Code analysis runs are configured for code projects in the project file for the code project. Code analysis runs are performed on the local computer. When you enable a code analysis check-in policy, files in a code project that are to be checked in must be compiled after their last edit. A code analysis run that contains, at a minimum, the rules in the team project settings must be performed on the computer where the changes have been made.

- For managed code, you set the check-in policy by specifying a rule set that contains a subset of the code analysis rules.

- For C/C++ code, the check-in policy requires that all code analysis rules are run. You can add preprocessor directives to disable specific rules for the individual code projects in your team project.

After you specify a check-in policy for managed code, team members can synchronize their code analysis settings for code projects to the team project policy settings.

# Refactoring

Code refactoring is the process of restructuring existing computer code—changing the factoring—without changing its external behavior. Refactoring improves nonfunctional attributes of the software. Advantages include improved code readability and reduced complexity; these can improve source code maintainability and create a more expressive internal architecture or object model to improve extensibility.

Typically, refactoring applies a series of standardized basic smaller refactorings, each of which is (usually) a tiny change in a computer program's source code that either preserves the behavior of the software, or at least does not modify its conformance to functional requirements. Many development environments provide automated support for performing the mechanical aspects of these basic refactorings. If done extremely well, code refactoring may also resolve hidden, dormant, or undiscovered computer bugs or vulnerabilities in the system by simplifying the underlying logic and eliminating unnecessary levels of complexity. If done poorly, it may fail the requirement that external functionality not be changed, and/or introduce new bugs.

Why do we use refactoring? Well, we want developers to constantly think about how they can keep the code simpler and more maintainable. We often do not need any gold plating on our code. As a PO, I am more interested in the value to the organization the code adds, not how cool or complicated it is.

# Pair Programming

Pair programming means that all code is produced by two people programming on one task on one computer. One programmer has control over the workstation (the driver) and is thinking mostly about the coding in detail. The other programmer is more focused on the big picture and is continually reviewing the code that is being produced by the first programmer. Programmers switch roles after a while so both will be in the driving seat at one time or another.

The pairs might not be fixed either. In many projects, programmers switch partners frequently, so that everyone knows what everyone is doing. This practice will also let everybody remain familiar with the whole system, even the parts outside their skill set. Doing this improves communication and cross-functionality of the team.

Why is this a good practice? Studies have shown that pair programming reduces bugs by somewhere between 15-50%. Reducing bugs by these numbers will lower the amount of time and effort you spend on chasing bugs in production.

Another benefit is that there are two pairs of eyes over the implementation of the requirement. The idea is that any misconceptions of the requirement the pair is working on quickly can be found since two persons collaborate to write the code. If there had been only a single developer writing the code, it would be harder to find such misconceptions. A single developer might also have written unit tests that are included in the continuous delivery model, which would be run successful since the tests are written by the same developer who wrote the code. This way, you would not see the misconceptions in your tests unless another set of eyes had reviewed the code.

Are there any drawbacks? Of course there are. One of the most discussed is that two programmers working at the same time cost twice as much than if only one developer does the job. This is true indeed. Here you need to consider the cost reduction of finding any defects early in the development process and not in production when the cost associated with fixing the defect is much greater. So a general rule is that we use pair programming on complicated features, important features, or high-risk features where we have higher quality standards than on some other code. Use it wisely, but don't be afraid to use it.

Another way to enhance code quality is to have peer review on important code. That is, a single developer writes the code and then sends a code review request to a peer to get someone else to look at the code. This is an effective way of working and does not require two full-time developers.

# Summary

This chapter focused on some of the most common agile practices. Many of them stem from Extreme Programming and are great quality enhancers for development projects. Visual Studio and TFS have great support for implementing these practices.

Keep in mind that these practices can be used in more "traditional" projects as well. They will help you increase quality in these projects as well.

The next chapter discusses some key metrics you can use to monitor the status of your agile projects.

■ ■ ■

# CHAPTER 7

# Metrics in Agile Projects

A *key performance indicator* (KPI) is a performance measurement used in most organizations to evaluate the organization's success or the success of a particular activity within the organization. Often, KPIs are used to measure the effects of a change project—for instance, implementing a good ALM process—or to evaluate the progress of a development project.

You can use the score from an ALM online assessment as a KPI and compare the assessment scores before and after the implementation of an ALM process improvement. This way, you get an indication of whether you have improved due to implementing a new process.

During projects, you should also be able to use the reports from your ALM toolset to determine whether you're constantly improving your work. Continuous improvement, in my opinion, is something to strive for. When it comes to project management, you can, for instance, look at the team's velocity (how fast the team is able to work) and see if it's growing or decreasing. By using reports and metrics from your ALM tools, you can choose the KPIs you want and learn how to evaluate them.

This chapter looks at metrics for five topics that cover most aspects of software development. Keep in mind that they are not only for agile projects but can be used in many other projects as well:

- Project management

- Architecture, analysis, and design

- Developer practices

- Software testing

- Release management

## Project-Management Metrics

To get good metrics about the status of your projects, it's important to measure your progress. You can do this in several ways. If you're using agile as a methodology, many of these metrics and reports should be familiar. To others, they may be new.

### Agile Metrics

Let's look at some important reports that are commonly used in agile practices:

- Backlog overview

- Sprint burndown

- Velocity report

- Release burndown

- Remaining work

- Unplanned work

The *backlog overview report* lists all user stories, filtered by tags and iteration and in order of importance. Basically this is a list of user stories filtered by the criteria you need. Many people use Excel (or an another spreadsheet application) to create this report, but many ALM tools have built-in support for producing it. Figure 7-1 shows what it will look like in VSTS.

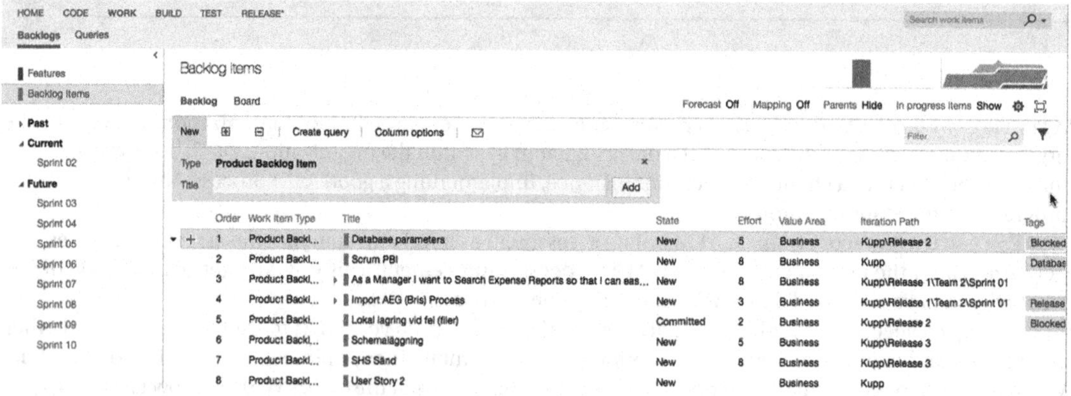

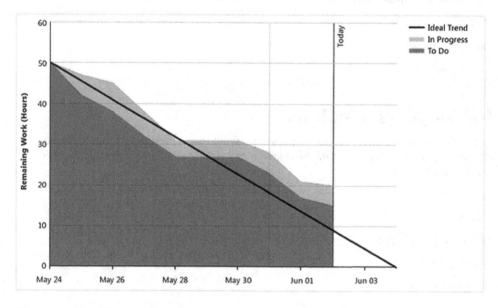

*Figure 7-1.* *The backlog overview in VSTS*

I've mentioned the *sprint burndown* chart before (see Figure 7-2). This report shows how much work there is left to do in a sprint. Using it, you can predict when the team will be finished with the work assigned to this sprint, either in the sprint or after the sprint is finished. Based on this information, the team and the product owner (PO) can take actions to make sure they deliver what they have committed to.

![Sprint burndown report chart showing Remaining Work (Hours) on the y-axis from 0 to 60 and dates from May 24 to Jun 03 on the x-axis, with legend for Ideal Trend, In Progress, and To Do]

*Figure 7-2.* *Sprint burndown report*

The *release burndown chart* (Figure 7-3) shows the same thing as the sprint burndown, but for the work included in a release.

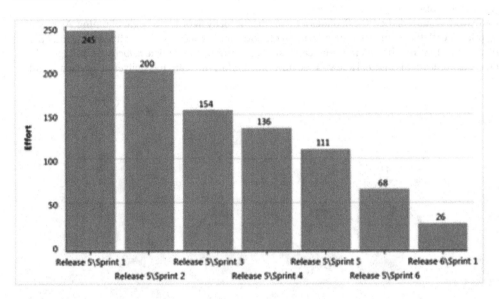

***Figure 7-3.*** *Release burndown report*

A *burndown and burn rate chart* (Figure 7-4) is another way to show a project's burndown. No surprises here: This is the same information shown in Figure 7-1. The burn rate summarizes the completed and required rate of work for a specified time period. In some tools, you can also see the information for team members. You can sometimes choose to see the report based on hours worked or number of work items.

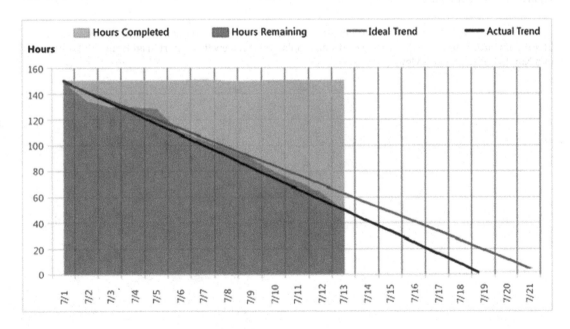

***Figure 7-4.*** *Burndown and burn rate report*

Velocity (how much work a team can take on in a sprint) is important, especially for a product owner (PO) planning who is how much work can be accomplished in coming sprints. Velocity is usually a measure of the effect per story point that the team can accomplish.

Before any work is started, the PO calculates a theoretical velocity in order to begin planning. As time goes by, it's updated with the team's real velocity based on how much work they deliver in each sprint. This helps the PO estimate how much work the team can take on in coming sprints. The *velocity chart* (Figure 7-5) can help you easily retrieve this figure. Here you see how much effort the team has delivered for each sprint.

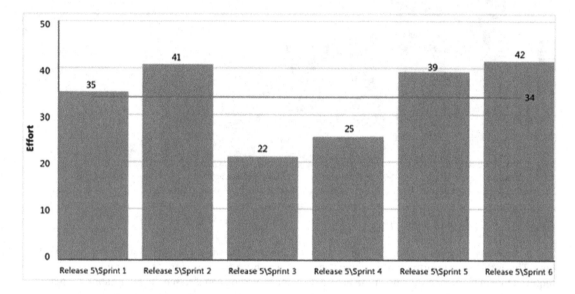

*Figure 7-5.* *Velocity report*

Rem*aining work* (Figure 7-6) is another great report. You can use it to track the team's progress and identify any problems in the flow of work. In some tools, you can view this report in an Hours of Work view or a Number of Work Items view.

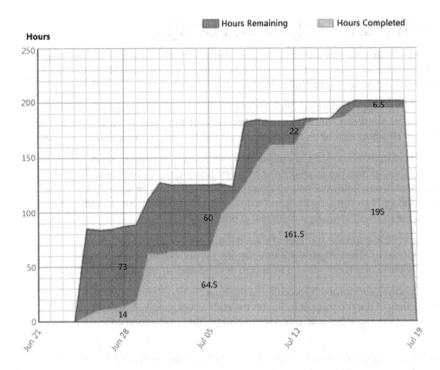

***Figure 7-6.*** *Remaining work report*

The *unplanned work report* (Figure 7-7) is useful when the team plans an iteration by identifying all work items that they intend to resolve or close during the course of the iteration. Work items assigned to the iteration by the plan completion date of the report are considered planned work. All work items that are added to the iteration after that date are identified as unplanned work.

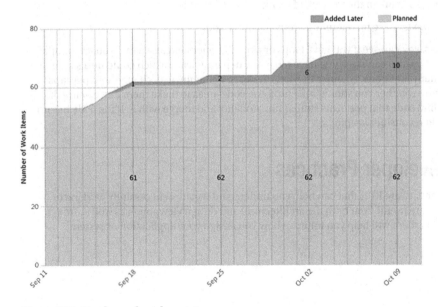

***Figure 7-7.*** *Unplanned work report*

# Metrics for Architecture, Analysis and Design

ALM tools don't include many metrics you can use for KPI assessment for architecture, but you can use some taken from the development area. Using the code metrics, you can get information about how your architecture and design are working, including the following:

- *Lines of code:* This is an approximate number based on Intermediate Language (IL) code. A high count may indicate that a type or method is doing too much work and should be split up. This may also be a warning that code will be hard to maintain.

- *Class coupling:* Measures the coupling to unique classes through parameters, local variables, return types, method calls, generic or template instantiations, base classes, interface implementations, fields defined on external types, and attribute decoration. Strive for low coupling; high coupling indicates a design that is difficult to reuse and maintain because of its many interdependencies on other types.

- *Depth of inheritance:* Indicates the number of class definitions that extend to the root of the class hierarchy. The deeper the hierarchy, the more difficult it may be to understand where particular methods and fields are defined and/or redefined.

- *Cyclomatic complexity:* Determined by calculating the number of different code paths in the flow of the program. It indicates the code's complexity. A high complexity makes maintainability suffer, and it can also be hard to get good code coverage.

- *Maintainability index:* An index value between 0 and 100 that represents the relative ease of maintaining the code. The higher the better: a rating above 60 is good. Below that, maintainability suffers.

Some ALM tools can generate dependency graphs. These graphs are used to visualize code and its relationships. Running analyzers on these graphs can give you useful information as well:

- *Circular references* are nodes that have circular dependencies on one another.

- *Hubs* are nodes that are in the top 25% of highly connected nodes.

- *Unreferenced nodes* have no references from any other nodes.

Using these analyzers, you can see if you have loops or circular dependencies so that you can simplify them or break the cycles. You also can see if you have too many dependencies, which could be a sign that they're performing too many functions. To make the code easier to maintain, test, change, and perhaps reuse, you need to look into whether you should refactor these code areas to make them more defined. You may also be able to find code that performs similar functionality and merge with it. If the code has no dependencies, you should reconsider keeping it.

# Metrics for Developer Practices

Metrics for developer practices are KPIs that can help you understand if you're successfully working to improve your code. These are useful from both the architectural and design viewpoints as well as from a developer viewpoint. Using them will help you improve how you design your application or system.

Several important metrics are available automatically in many tools and can help you get a good understanding of the quality of your development work:

- Code coverage
- Code metrics
- Compiler warnings
- Code analysis warnings

## Code Coverage

Code coverage shows you how much of the code has been covered by automated unit tests. You get the value as a percentage of the entire codebase. The difficulty often is deciding what percentage is enough. Should you always strive for 100%, or is 80% enough? This is something the team has to discuss with the PO in Scrum or a similar decision-maker in other processes. This value is input for the Definition of Done (DoD).

## Code Metrics

You can look at several different code metrics:

- *Lines of code* is an approximate number based on IL code. A high count may indicate that a type or method is doing too much work and should be split up. This may also be a warning that code will be difficult to maintain.

- *Class coupling* measures coupling to unique classes through parameters, local variables, return types, method calls, generic or template instantiations, base classes, interface implementations, fields defined on external types, and attribute decoration. You should strive for low coupling because high coupling indicates a design that is difficult to reuse and maintain due to of its many interdependencies on other types.

- *Depth of inheritance* indicates the number of class definitions that extend to the root of the class hierarchy. The deeper the hierarchy, the more difficult it may be to understand where particular methods and fields are defined and/or redefined.

- *Cyclomatic complexity* is determined by calculating the number of different code paths in the flow of the program; it shows the complexity of the code. High complexity makes maintainability suffer and can also make it difficult to achieve good code coverage.

- The *maintainability index* is an index value between 0 and 100 that represents the relative ease of maintaining the code. The higher the better. A rating above 60 is good. Below that, maintainability suffers.

## Compiler Warnings

Errors and warnings should be avoided in a project. Allowing more than zero errors or warnings tends to result in the team accepting lower quality in the codebase, which over time causes the code to lose maintainability (commonly known as the *broken windows theory*[1]).

Track this metric to make sure the number of errors is zero. This should ideally be enforced by automatic build policies.

---

[1]See http://en.wikipedia.org/wiki/Broken_windows_theory.

## Code Analysis Warnings

Code analysis in development tools performs static analysis on code, which helps developers identify potential design, globalization, interoperability, performance, security, and many other categories of potential problems. Much of this is so far only available for .NET development; if you're using Java, things may be different.

Code analysis tools provide warnings that indicate rule violations in managed code libraries. The warnings are organized into rule areas such as design, localization, performance, and security. Each warning signifies a violation of a code analysis rule.

Code analysis can be used to enforce company policies on the code developers write. Many ALM tools offer good support for code analysis, usually including a set of rules. Often you can even extend them by writing your own rule set or suppress the rules you don't want. Definitely discuss this with your development team and the PO, because the warnings have an impact on the effort required before the DoD is fulfilled.

# Metrics for Software Testing

Software testing is an important area. Testing should be a constant part of any development effort and not only a phase at the end of the project. There are good metrics you can use during your projects to make sure you have high-quality testing in place.

Following are a number of metrics you can use as KPIs for software testing:

- *Number of bugs per state:* How many bugs are active, resolved, or closed? Is the number of active bugs increasing and the number of resolved and closed bugs constant? If so, you need to look into how you perform your testing.

- *Number of bugs sent back from testers for more information (AKA, reactivated bugs):* A large number may indicate that communication between developers and testers must improve.

- *Code coverage:* This shows how much of the code has been covered by automated unit tests. You get the value as a percentage of the entire codebase.

- *Tests run results:* How are your tests performing? Do you have many failed tests? If so, what can you do to improve this?

- *Percent requirements covered by test cases:* Do you write test cases for all your requirements? If not, what is the reason?

- *Percent requirements covered by testing:* Do you actually run the tests for which you have test cases? If this figure is low and the figure for *percent requirements covered by test cases* is high, you may have an issue you need to deal with.

## Example Reports

The metrics you get in your reports concerning testing can be very helpful in your projects. The reports described here are found in many tools:

- Bug status

- Reactivations

- Bug trend

# Bug Status Report

The *bug status report* gives you information about the cumulative bug count based on bug state, priority, who it's assigned to, and, of course, bug severity. It shows you the number of bugs and the number of resolved bugs (see Figures 7-8 and 7-9).

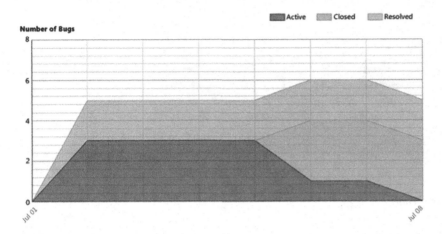

*Figure 7-8. Bug status report*

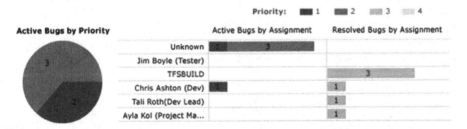

*Figure 7-9. Bug status report*

Figure 7-8 shows the number of bugs over time. You can see how the numbers of active, closed, and resolved bugs have changed. In this case, the number of active bugs is decreasing and the number of closed and resolved bugs is increasing, leading to a point where the number of active bugs is zero.

Figure 7-9 shows a report that displays how many bugs are assigned to an individual user. You can also see the priority of each bug as well as how many bugs have been resolved by the users.

# Reactivations Report

The *reactivations report* (see Figure 7-10) is used to see how many bugs have been resolved or closed too early. If a bug needs to be opened again, it's called a *reactivation*. A high number indicates that the developers need to improve their bug-fixing process and not close or resolve the bugs unless they really are ready to be closed. It can also be an indication that you have bad communication between testers and developers. For instance, incomplete test reports and poorly written test cases can cause this.

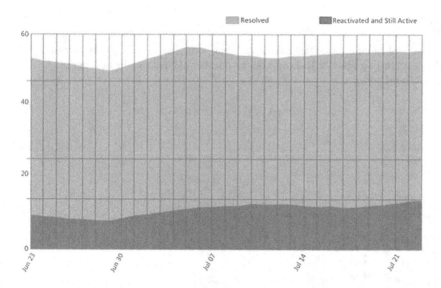

*Figure 7-10.* *Reactivations report*

## Bug Trend Report

Next is the *bug trend report* (see Figure 7-11). This report helps you track the rate at which your team is finding, resolving, and closing bugs.

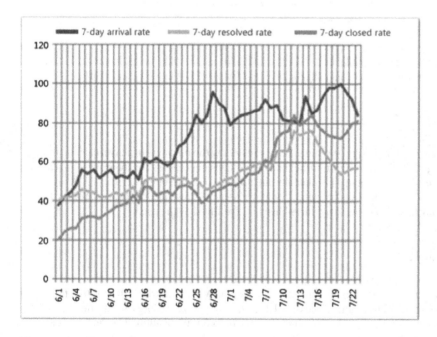

*Figure 7-11.* *Bug trend report*

# Metrics for Release Management

A quick look at the Information Technology Infrastructure Library (ITIL) (`www.itilnews.com/ITIL_v3_Suggested_Release_and_Deployment_KPIs.html`) will give you some other KPIs you can use. If you want to use them, you may need to create your own reports to automate the retrieval of this information. ITIL mentions these KPIs, among others:

- Number of software defects in production, which is the number of bugs or software defects of applications (versions) that are in production

- Percentage of successful software upgrades, which excludes full installations

- Number of untested releases (not tested and signed off)

- Number of urgent releases

- Average costs of release, where costs most likely are based on man-hours spent

---

■ **Note** The ITIL is a set of practices for IT service management (ITSM) that focuses on aligning IT services with the needs of business. ITIL describes procedures, tasks, and checklists that aren't organization specific, and are used by organizations to establish a minimum level of competency. It allows an organization to establish a baseline from which it can plan, implement, and measure. It's used to demonstrate compliance and to measure improvement.

---

## Sample Reports

Following the progress of your builds is essential in order to keep track of quality. These reports differ from ALM platform to platform, but let's look at some examples from Microsoft Team Foundation Server 2012. Use them as inspirations for what you can look for in your platform:

- Build quality indicators

- Build success over time

- Build summary report

The *build quality indicators report* (see Figure 7-12) shows a summary of some important values for your builds. Using this data, you can see whether you're close to releasing the build. Some of the information this report shows includes the following:

- *Active bugs:* How many active bugs existed at the time of the build.

- *Code churn:* The number of lines of code that have been added, removed, and changed in the check-ins before the build.

- *Code coverage:* Percentage of code covered by tests.

- *Inconclusive tests:* The number of tests that didn't succeed or were paused. If the build didn't succeed, the tests are either not counted or counted as inconclusive.

- *Failed tests:* How many tests failed during the build.

- *Passed tests:* How many tests were passed during the build.

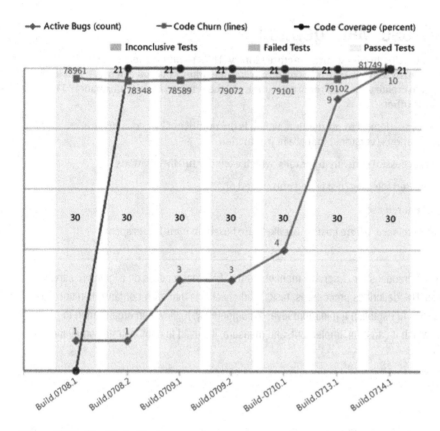

**Figure 7-12.** *Quality indicators report*

The *build success over time* report (see Figure 7-13) shows you the status of the last build for each build category (a combination of build definition, platform, and configuration) that runs each day. You can use this report to help you keep track of the quality of the code that you check in. Furthermore, for any day on which a build ran, you can view the build summary for that specific day.

| Build Definition | Platform | Configuration | No Build | Build Failed | Build Succeeded, No Tests | Tests Failed | Tests Passed, Low Coverage | Passed |
|---|---|---|---|---|---|---|---|---|

| Build Definition | Platform | Configuration | 6/2 | 6/3 | 6/4 | 6/5 | **6/6** | **6/7** | 6/8 | 6/9 | 6/10 | **6/11** | **6/12** | 6/13 | **6/14** | 6/15 |
|---|---|---|---|---|---|---|---|---|---|---|---|---|---|---|---|---|
| AllDebug | x86 | Debug | | | | | | | | | | | | | | |
| DebugAnyCPU | Any CPU | Debug | | | | | | | | | | | | | | |
| Debugx86 | x86 | Debug | | | | | | | | | | | | | | |
| ReleaseAnyCPU | Any CPU | Release | | | | | | | | | | | | | | |
| Releasex86 | x86 | Release | | | | | | | | | | | | | | |

**Figure 7-13.** *Build success over time report*

The *build summary* report (see Figure 7-14) shows you information about test results, test coverage, and code churn, as well as quality notes for each build.

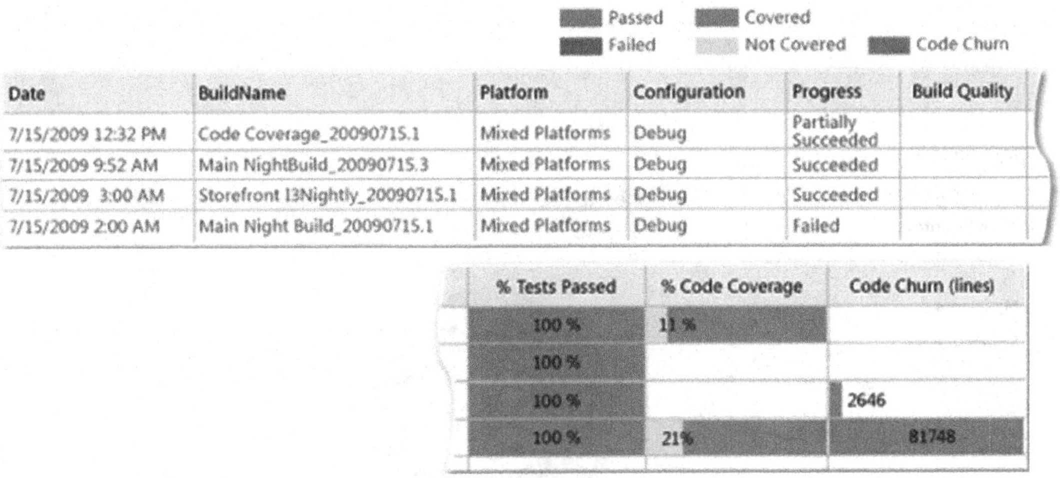

| Date | BuildName | Platform | Configuration | Progress | Build Quality |
|------|-----------|----------|---------------|----------|---------------|
| 7/15/2009 12:32 PM | Code Coverage_20090715.1 | Mixed Platforms | Debug | Partially Succeeded | |
| 7/15/2009 9:52 AM | Main NightBuild_20090715.3 | Mixed Platforms | Debug | Succeeded | |
| 7/15/2009 3:00 AM | Storefront I3Nightly_20090715.1 | Mixed Platforms | Debug | Succeeded | |
| 7/15/2009 2:00 AM | Main Night Build_20090715.1 | Mixed Platforms | Debug | Failed | |

| % Tests Passed | % Code Coverage | Code Churn (lines) |
|----------------|-----------------|--------------------|
| 100 % | 11 % | |
| 100 % | | |
| 100 % | | 2646 |
| 100 % | 21% | 81748 |

*Figure 7-14. Build summary report*

These metrics are suggestions that you can use as a base for following up on progress and quality in your projects. Different ALM tools offer different possibilities for reporting and collecting information. Thus it's important that you think through what you want for your organization when choosing an ALM platform.

# Using Charts to Monitor Metrics

In TFS you can also add charts to monitor information about your projects. In Figure 7-15, you can see that the charts can be created if you navigate to Queries and then select charts. You can create charts from many queries that you create using the query editor.

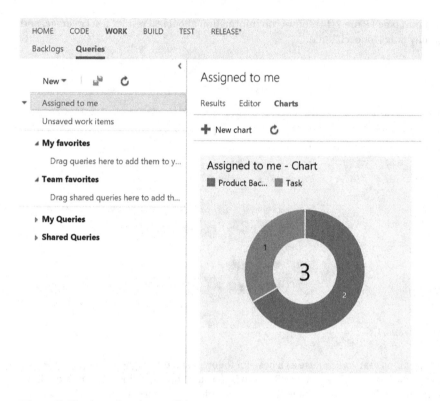

**Figure 7-15.** *Accessing charts editing*

You can choose to create many types of charts (Figure 7-16) including pie, bar, column, stacked bar, and so on, so that you can display the results as you want. If you create a chart that will be useful to the whole team, you can add that chart to the project home page so that it will always show up when you open the web portal. For this to work, you must create the query as a shared query.

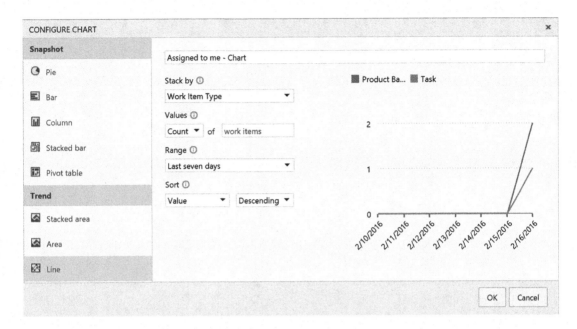

*Figure 7-16. Charts can be displayed in various ways*

With TFS 2015 Update 2, you can add charts for work item queries to the dashboard from the widget catalog. These charts are configurable. You can choose a query and a chart type, as well as visualization options while staying in the dashboard context. Chart types include pie, bar, column, stacked bar, line, area, and stacked area. You can also display data in a pivot table. And, you can still add charts from the Charts tab in the Work hub and configure them just like you've always done.

# Summary

Metrics and KPIs are valuable for any organization if you want to evaluate progress and quality. This chapter has shown some examples of metrics you can use for your agile projects, but they are not limited to these projects. They can help you run your projects more efficiently and with higher application quality as an end result.

Keep in mind that different organizations find different metrics valuable. This chapter has given examples of metrics that are commonly used, but there may be others that are better suited for you.

The next chapter walks you through a scenario that implements agile processes on different levels in a software development project.

# CHAPTER 8

■ ■ ■

# Agile Project Management in TFS

This chapter follows the startup of an agile project using VSTS. Many of the concepts covered earlier in the book are exemplified in this chapter, so you can see how to move from planning to implementation. The chapter also looks at how VSTS can support the agile project management process during sprints.

Keep in mind that although we use VSTS as an example, you can do most of the things shown here (and then some) in an on-premise TFS.

This chapter uses a fictitious company in the examples. This way you use a common denominator in the things you present so you can more easily understand the process and how TFS/VSTS supports our development organization.

This chapter focuses on the project management parts of a project. Support for agile development practices such as continuous integration, test-driven development, test automation, and so on, will be explained in subsequent chapters.

The main part of this chapter is written from the perspective of the product owner (PO), whom you will meet shortly. There will be a personal touch to some parts. This is because part of a project focuses on collaboration and interaction between people.

## Case Study

Let's start with the company used as an example. Any similarities to real companies are entirely unintentional.

### Company Background

Fabrikam Fiber provides cable television and related services to the United States. They are growing rapidly and have embraced Windows Azure to scale their customer-facing web site directly to end users to allow them to self-service tickets and track technicians. They also use an on-premises ASP.NET Model-View-Controller (MVC) application for their customer service representatives to administer customer orders.

Fabrikam development manager, Cindy Crafoord, has decided to implement a pilot project using the ALM features of TFS/VSTS to bridge the gap between what they have today and what they can benefit from in TFS/VSTS 2012. If the pilot is successful, Fabrikam will migrate all its development to the TFS/VSTS platform.

Cindy and Bob Peak (the IT manager) have decided to use Scrum as the preferred project management method, and the developers agree on using XP practices to enhance the quality of the software and therefore increase business value to the company.

© Joachim Rossberg 2016
J. Rossberg, *Agile Project Management using Team Foundation Server 2015*,
DOI 10.1007/978-1-4842-1870-9_8

## The Pilot Project

The project Fabrikam decided to use as a pilot for the ALM implementation is an expense-reporting application (Fabrikam Expense Reporting). In the early days, expenses were handled easily by the administrative staff, but since the company has grown quickly and salespeople are located and traveling all over the United States, things have become a little more complicated. The admin staff wants an application that will make their jobs easier and at the same time make sure employees will get reimbursed for expenses quickly. The requirements for this application are covered in the section "Requirements" later in this chapter.

Because this project will be using Scrum as a project-management process, Cindy and Bob have appointed Fiona Gallos as PO for the application. Fiona has only been working with Fabrikam for six months. She is experienced as a PO because her previous employer used Scrum extensively. Fiona also has PO certification from both Scrum Alliance and Scrum.org.

Important stakeholders for the project are Bob Peak, Cindy Crafoord, and Karen Guckenheimer. Karen is manager for the admin department and will represent the end users as well as the admin organization. Because the project aims to be a pilot program for an ALM implementation, Dave Applemust from the infrastructure side and Harry Bryan from the development organization are also considered important stakeholders.

### The People

- Alice Miller, CEO

- Bob Peak, IT manager

- Cindy Crafoord, development manager

- Karen Guckenheimer, admin manager

- Dave Applemust, infrastructure specialist

- Eric Parrot, business analyst

- Fiona Gallos, product owner

- Guillio Peters, Scrum master

- Harry Bryan, senior developer

- Mikael Persbrandt, developer

- Petter Ivarsson, user experience (UX)

- Ingrid Svensson, senior tester

# Scrum Process

Fiona and her co-workers selected the Scrum process for their project. This process is supplied out of the box by Microsoft and is a good implementation of Scrum. Chapter 3 covered what work items are available in the Scrum process.

# TFS/VSTS Web Portal

A TFS/VSTS web portal is created for all new TFS/VSTS projects (Figure 8-1).

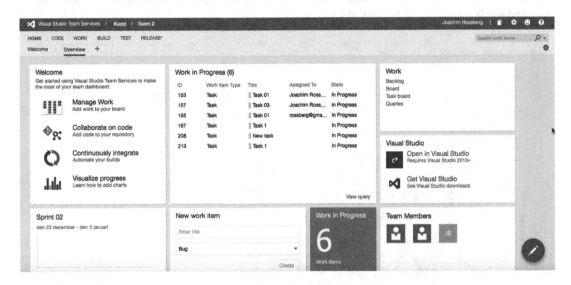

***Figure 8-1.*** *VSTS web access is similar to the access in the on-premise TFS*

You can use the TFS/VSTS web portal if you want to let non-technical users add reports of bugs or new product backlog items (PBIs). From this, you can view reports, create new work items, view builds, and much more. Often the PO or SM prefers to use the portal so he or she doesn't have to use Visual Studio to access these features. If you have a PO or SM who prefers a Mac, web access is the best way to access the power of TFS/VSTS.

You can set access control for the web access in Settings for the project. By controlling the access to the portal, you can let certain users or groups of users only see (and do) what you want them to see. This way, you can let customers (if you are a consultant) into TFS/VSTS with limited functionality. The portal is great for different kinds of collaboration.

In the web portal we can find quick links to important information in our project. We can directly see the work in progress for the current sprint. We can also add new work items directly from the start page. Many aspects of the welcome page are customizable so we can tailor it in ways that will be of use for our project. We can add information here about our builds, bugs, impediments, and much more so we can provide a good overview for team members and stakeholders alike. Below Work we find links to the backlog, the Scrum board, work items, and so on. We can also see a list of the team members who are part of our project. Keep in mind that if you are using VSTS the look and feel of the web portal can change whenever Microsoft implements new functionality (every three weeks).

## Charts and Queries

There are a few out-of-the-box charts with the templates in TFS/VSTS. Let's just say that the burndown chart (Figure 8-2) is the most common status report used. The burndown shows how many hours are still left in the sprint and is useful to determine if you are on track.

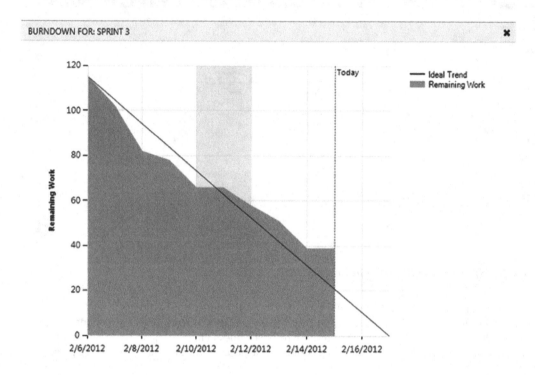

*Figure 8-2.* *The burndown chart*

There are also queries you can use to retrieve information from TFS/VSTS: One query that is always supplied in the Scrum template is the "Assigned to Me" query (Figure 8-3), which shows all of the work items assigned to me.

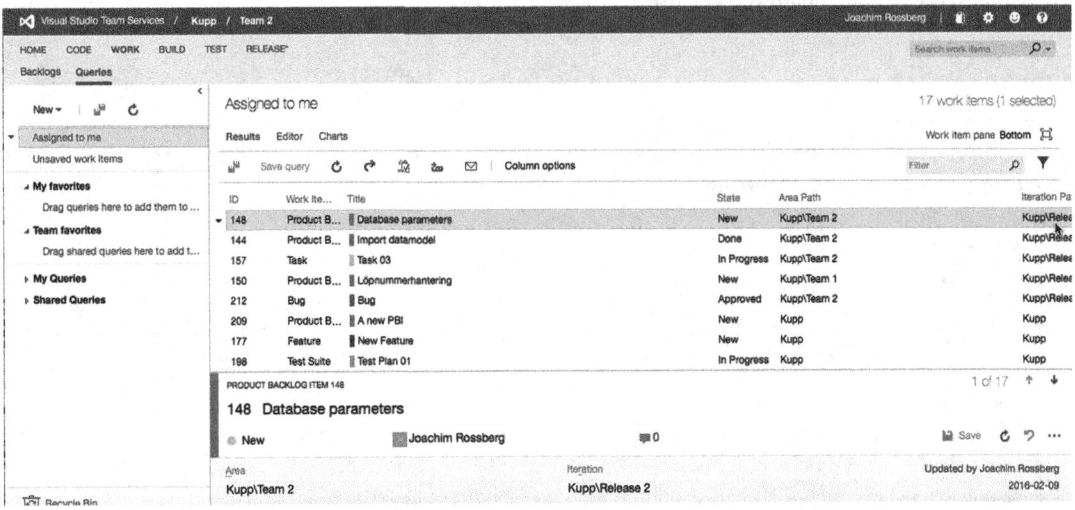

***Figure 8-3.*** *The Assigned to Me query in TFS/VSTS*

Using Work Item Query Language (WIQL) (Figure 8-4), you can modify or write new queries that suit you better. You can do this by using the built-in WIQL Editor. Check out `http://msdn.microsoft.com/en-us/library/bb130198(v=vs.90).aspx` for more information about WIQL.

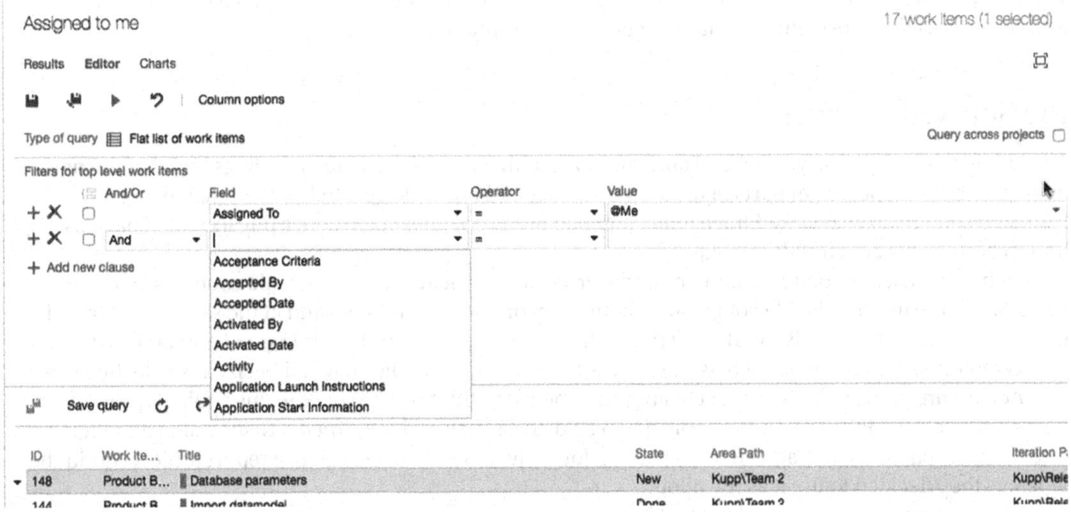

***Figure 8-4.*** *Modifying the Assigned to Me query in TFS/VSTS*

In TFS/VSTS, you can use an electronic task board to show the state of the work items on the sprint backlog (Figure 8-5). Here, you can see what has been done, what is in progress, and so on, instead of using sticky notes on a wall! Having a big (touch-sensitive) screen on the wall that shows progress provides all of the team members with up-to-date information, not to mention the PO when he or she visits the team room. There is also the Kanban board you can use.

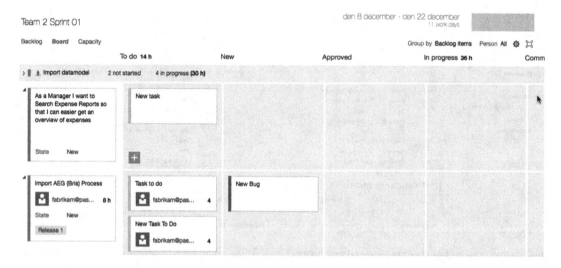

***Figure 8-5.*** *The task board showing sprint backlog items and their status in TFS/VSTS*

# Project Startup Phase

This section follows the PO, Fiona Gallos, during the startup phase of the project. You will see how TFS/VSTS is used to insert the information Fiona collects during this phase.

## PO Sets Off to Work

The idea for this project started when Fabrikam noticed that bug fixes created new bugs and that the new bugs sometimes appeared in parts of the system considered not to be affected by the original bug fix. Fabrikam soon realized it lacked traceability and had no way of knowing where a bug fix would have its impact besides the actual code change.

Fiona had just attended a conference and learned a great deal about ALM, agile concepts, and TFS/VSTS. She came up with the idea of getting a better grip on the ALM process and at the same time started using agile practices at Fabrikam. Both of these efforts could greatly improve things at Fabrikam so it could avoid embarrassing situations such as when customers found new bugs that had been caused by bug fixes.

At the same time, Fiona saw that collaboration between the two developer teams could improve if they started to use TFS/VSTS. Fiona wrote down a business case and presented it to the management team. After a few discussions they agreed to try it as a pilot project. Because the expense report project was in the pipeline, they decided to use it as the pilot.

At this point it was hard to calculate ROI, but anything that could improve how the customers viewed them would be worth the effort.

# Building the Initial Team

It is recommended that the PO starts with a small team during initial planning of the project. Fiona selected Cindy Crafoord, Harry Bryan, and Eric Parrot because they were experienced within the company and were also senior members with experience from other companies as well. They were also available for the whole pilot project, which was an important aspect for Fiona. She knew the importance of having consistency among the team members during a project. Guillio Peters would be the SM for the entire project. The rest of the team would be selected a bit later in the project.

Fiona created the project in VSTS (Figure 8-6) from the web portal using the Scrum template. She named it Fabrikam Pilot, chose Scrum, and also used Git Version Control. The team had discussed which version control to use, Git or Team Foundation Version Control, and decided to go for the former.

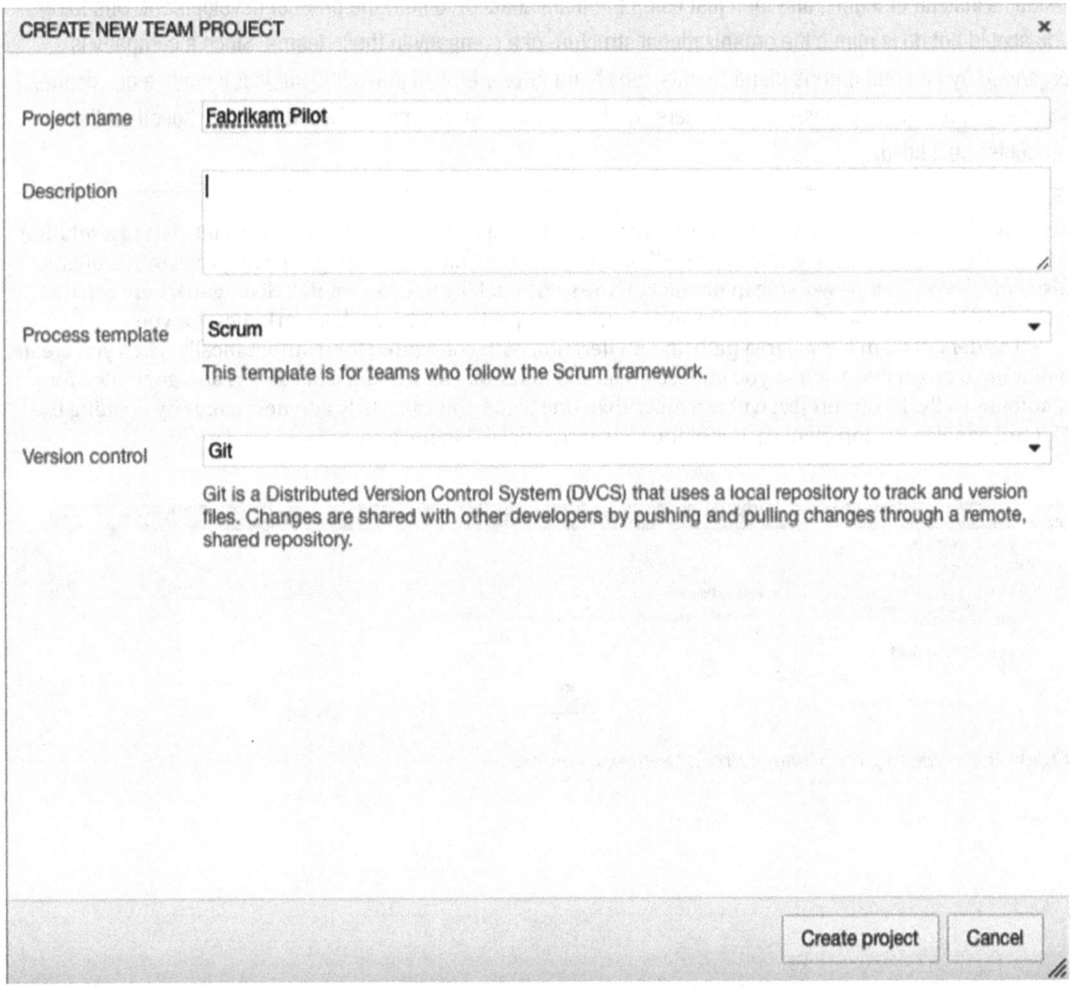

| CREATE NEW TEAM PROJECT | ✕ |
|---|---|
| Project name | Fabrikam Pilot |
| Description | |
| Process template | Scrum ▾ |
| | This template is for teams who follow the Scrum framework. |
| Version control | Git ▾ |
| | Git is a Distributed Version Control System (DVCS) that uses a local repository to track and version files. Changes are shared with other developers by pushing and pulling changes through a remote, shared repository. |
| | Create project    Cancel |

*Figure 8-6. Creating the Fabrikam Pilot project in TFS/VSTS*

Then she started to create the teams necessary for the project.

# Creating New Teams

In VSTS, a team is simply a way of recognizing the team or teams you have, whether that is one team working on a project or several. One person can be a member of several teams. Using area paths, you can describe what development work belongs to a specific team. You can easily look at what work items belong to the team that they are responsible for. If a work item is assigned to an area path that is assigned to a team, that work item is placed into the backlog for that team.

---

■ **Note**    A *team* is a concept used by Microsoft, but won't necessarily match something in your organization. A team can be anything and it can also represent your product. It can be easier for the users to think about products instead of teams, and then just using the team concept to staff the product development. One thing you should not do is mimic the organizational structure of a company in these teams. Since a company is organized by different criteria (departments, which are further broken down into subject teams), a development team for a product may cross these borders. That means that the teams discussed here are based on the products you'll build.

---

There are several ways you can use teams. Some let a specific team work on a specific part of a solution while another team work on other parts, all having a separate backlog. In large Scrum projects you might also need several teams working in parallel on the same backlog but you want to distinguish between the teams and the work they do. The best way is to try it in a project and see what works best for you.

The default team has an area path and an iteration path configured for it automatically when you create a new team project. As soon as you choose areas and iterations for a team, a backlog is also generated for it automatically. If your project will use more than one team, you can easily add new teams by opening the Control panel in the top-right corner of the web access page (Figure 8-7).

***Figure 8-7.***  *Opening the Manage Project Settings window*

In the Project Profile view (Figure 8-8), you can create a new team by clicking on the New Team link.

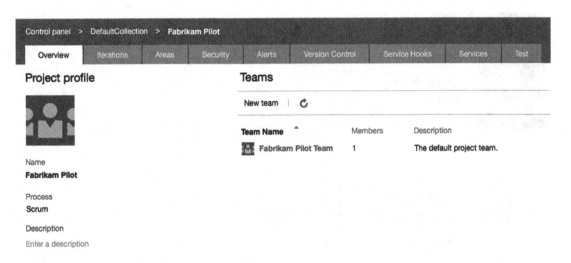

***Figure 8-8.*** *Creating a new team from the Project Profile page*

Fill in all information about the team (Figure 8-9). In this screen you can also select permissions for the team by adding the team to an existing security group (more about this in a later section). You can also create a team area at this time, but if you don't you can associate it with an area later. When you are done, click Create Team. In a few seconds the new team is created and you can start adding users to it.

CREATE NEW TEAM                                                                    ✕

# PROFILE  SETTINGS

Team name

Fabrikam Program Team

Description

Permissions

You can add your team to any existing security group to automatically inherit permissions.

[Fabrikam Pilot]\Project Administrators                                            ▼

Team area

☐ Create an area path with the name of the team.

Create team    Cancel

*Figure 8-9.* *Entering values for the new team*

## The Backlog and Team Structure for the Fabrikam Pilot

Fiona will have two development teams working on the project. They will both work from a common backlog managed by the Fabrikam Program Team. However, each team does not have to see each others PBIs but instead wants a subset of the program backlog in their team backlog. Figure 8-10 shows an overview of this structure.

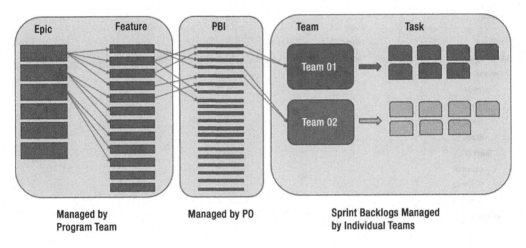

**Figure 8-10.** *The backlog structure*

To accomplish this, Fiona first creates three teams:

- Fabrikam Program Team

- Fabrikam Team 01

- Fabrikam Team 02

Fiona will then configure areas and iterations to accommodate this structure of the backlog. Fiona creates three areas that do not differ from the team structure; each team is associated with its respective area in VSTS:

- Fabrikam Program Team

- Fabrikam Team 01

- Fabrikam Team 02

She then continues to configure the initial sprint structure. So far in the project she has no estimates and cannot decide the complete release and sprint structure. But she knows she will have several releases and that each release will have its own sprints. Knowing she can change this structure, she creates the iteration structure shown in Figure 8-11.

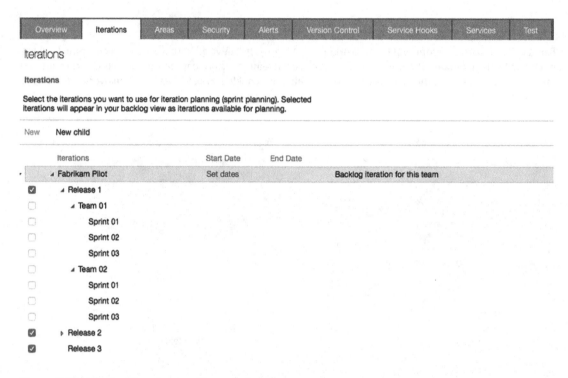

**Figure 8-11.** *The iteration structure Fiona starts with*

For each of the teams, she selects the appropriate iterations that they will see in their backlogs. Figure 8-11 shows that the program team will be able to plan on a release level, for instance.

By using areas and iterations in this way, Fiona was able to implement the structure she wanted. Keep in mind that you can use areas and iterations in many ways; this is only one way to use it.

## Building the Teams

Now the team was close to getting started. Fiona had Cindy Crafoord, Harry Bryan, Eric Parrot, and Guillio Peters in the team so far. She talked to the other team members and they decided they needed three more people to enhance the development and testing competences even more. She also got feedback from the initial team that they needed an experienced UX person onboard. They selected the following:

- Mikael Persbrandt, developer

- Ingrid Svensson, senior tester

- Petter Ivarsson, UX

She was also able to select four other persons who would work on Team 02. Fiona then contacted each person's manager and made sure he or she would be available for the project. Luckily, they all were, and when she approached the potential team members, they were happy to come aboard.

Fiona suggested two-week sprints because that was a good time box based on her experience. She once had a team who complained that they could not finish their PBIs during the four-week sprints they used. They always seemed to be late or failed to deliver everything they had committed to, complaining they needed more time in the sprints. She then said, "Okay, then we use two-week sprints instead." The team was very confused, as Fiona had decreased the number of days in the sprints, not increased them. Once they started working on the two-week sprints, however, they soon found they delivered more in two weeks than they had in four weeks. The team was more focused and did not postpone anything until the end of the sprint, hence, they were more effective.

With the team in place, Fiona was ready to start sprint planning. Let's first look at how you could use TFS/VSTS to manage the team.

One part of the responsibilities of the PO is to staff the project, at least initially. After an initial team is created, it is up to the team members to inform the PO about which competences they need to fulfill the project vision.

This chapter looks further into how you can create and build teams in VSTS. It will show how you can add new team members, create new teams, and set user access rights to team members. You will also see how team members can set up alerts so that they can be notified when important events occur. Such an event could be that they have a work item assigned to them or that a work item they created has changed. This chapter is more hands-on than Chapter 5 and gives you direct instruction for managing your team.

# Adding Team Members

Once the project is created, navigate to the web access front page. One team is created by default so you can start adding members right away. However, it could be good practice to consider creating teams other than the default team so that you get more flexibility in how you manage the project. You will see more on how to create teams later in the chapter, but now you will focus on adding members to the default team. Click on the Team Members link, as shown in Figure 8-12.

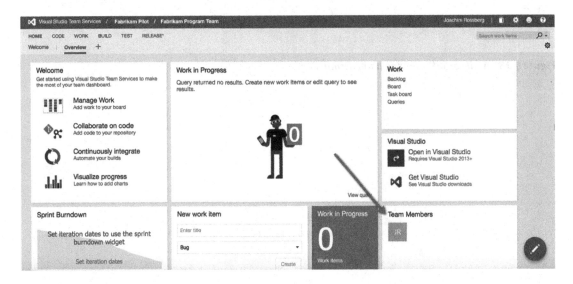

*Figure 8-12. Managing team members*

This will open the window shown in Figure 8-13. From this screen, you can add or remove team members and team groups.

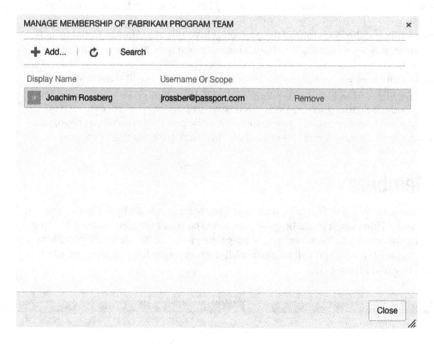

*Figure 8-13.* *Adding and removing team members*

# Managing VSTS Groups, Teams, and User's Permission

From the Control Panel, you can change permissions for both teams and team groups by going to the Security tab (Figure 8-14) and selecting the group's tab.

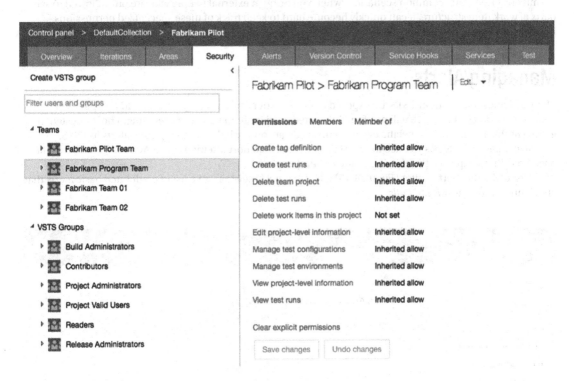

*Figure 8-14.* *Viewing permissions for groups and teams from the Control Panel*

You can see that there are six different VSTS groups by default:

- *Build Administrators*: Members of this group have build permissions for the project. Members can manage test environments, create test runs, and manage builds.

- *Contributors*: Members of this group can contribute to the project. This means they can add, modify, and delete code, and create and modify work items. By default, the team group created when you create a team project is added to this group. Therefore, any user you add to the team will be a member of this group.

- *Project Administrators*: Members of this group can administer the team project. However, they cannot create projects.

- *Project Valid Users*: Members of this group have access to VSTS. This group automatically contains all users and groups that have been added anywhere within VSTS. You cannot modify the membership of this group.

- *Readers*: Members of this group can view the project. They may not modify it.

- *Release Administrators*: Members of this group can perform all operations on release management.

There are various permissions you can set for the groups and team members. This chapter does not go over all of them, so refer to the TFS documentation if you need more info. `http://msdn.microsoft.com/en-us/library/vstudio/ms252587.aspx` is a good place to start.

Note that by default most permissions are inherited. You can break the inheritance and define custom permissions here. One common scenario is when you bring in external people who are only allowed to see parts of work item structure. It can quickly become hard to keep track of these specialized permissions, however, so use them with care.

# Managing Alerts

Many activities that occur in VSTS are exposed as events. For example, every time a build completes or changeset is checked in, VSTS will notify all interested parties about this. As a user I might be interested in getting notifications when a specific event occurs. I can accomplish this by configuring alerts in VSTS.

To configure the alerts you use the Alert Editor in the web portal settings page. You can also access this page from Team Explorer, by selecting Team and Project Alerts.

First of all, the Alerts Editor (Figure 8-15) lets you quickly select from a list of predefined basic alerts that are common, such as *A Build Fails*.

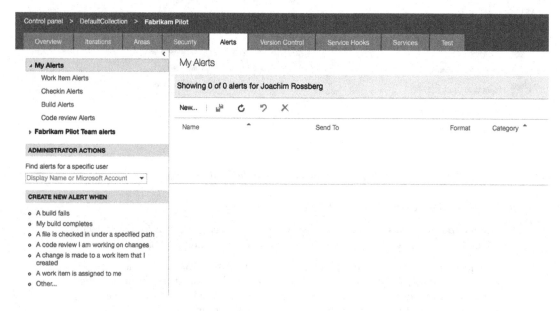

***Figure 8-15.*** *Selecting an alert in the Alerts Editor*

Select the New Alerts drop-down to create more advanced alerts (Figure 8-16). This tab shows your existing personal alerts (Scope My Alert) and the team alerts and lets you select from a list of templates when creating a new alert.

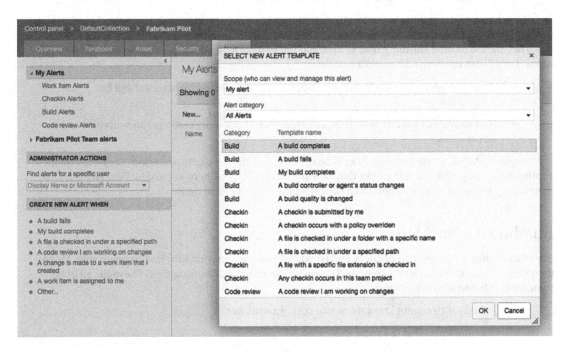

***Figure 8-16.*** *Selecting a custom alert in the Alerts Editor*

We will now continue following Fiona. Fiona had done everything to build an initial product backlog and create the team. At this point she does not have any input as to how long the project will take or how much it will cost. In order to get this information so she can show it to the stakeholders, there are a few steps she needs to take. Let's take a look at these because this will also involve planning the first sprint.

# Requirements

Requirements gathering was the fun part of the project in Fiona's eyes. Discussions with traditional project managers and stakeholders about requirements always came up, and she enjoyed that. Traditionally all requirements had to be determined at the beginning of the project, and it was hard for many to accept that it is okay to start a project even without specifying everything. The fact that so many of these requirements were wrong or unnecessary in the end didn't seem to bother traditionalists. They still went head first into projects that often failed or were flawed.

Fiona had run so many successful agile projects she knew that catching higher-level requirements in the beginning was okay. They could start without all of the details because they would be clarified at each sprint planning meeting and also during the sprints.

Fiona called the initial team together for a requirements workshop. She also added Karen Guckenheimer to the workshop because she was one of the main stakeholders from the business side. Because Guillio (SM) was not present, Fiona explained what they were going to do. She stressed that they should look for higher-level requirements in the sense that they did not have to detail them yet. There would not be any discussions about solutions or technicalities at this point. That would be left for the development team to decide when the sprints started.

To avoid any confusion, she then explained the concept of a user story to the requirements team. Fiona wanted all requirements in this form:

*As a <type of user>, I want <some goal> so that <some reason>.*

Fiona had calculated three hours for this meeting and booked a room with a large whiteboard. She also supplied sticky notes and pens for everyone.

They started by brainstorming user stories, and things were a bit slow to begin. The meeting took off when Harry Bryan came up with two user stories:

- As a sales person, I want to manage expense reports over the Internet so I can be more efficient.

- As a manager, I want to search expense reports so I can more easily get an overview of expenses.

Suddenly they all started writing. After little over an hour, the pace dropped again. They then spent another hour going over the user stories they had and clarified any of them as needed. Fiona felt they had done a great job so far and had a good foundation for the work ahead of them.

## Building the Backlog

After the meeting, Fiona went to her desk and typed in a spreadsheet what they had come up with. Fiona then started to order the list by dragging and dropping the PBIs in the backlog view. She made an initial prioritization based on some assumptions:

- Initially they cannot know the actual cost of a work item.

- All work items cost the same to develop.

- Prioritization will be based on importance only.

- After initial sprint planning and estimation, the list will be updated again.

It took Fiona roughly 30 minutes to complete the initial sorting. Now she really had something to start with. It was still early afternoon and she wanted to add the user stories to TFS/VSTS before going home for the day.

## Adding Backlog Items in TFS/VSTS

Fiona opened the project web access in Safari and felt a little bit of excitement as she saw the empty project that soon would be filled with activities. She had lots of input for the backlog.

She took a long look at the results of the initial story writing workshop she had in front of her and started by going to the Backlogs tab on the web page (Figure 8-17).

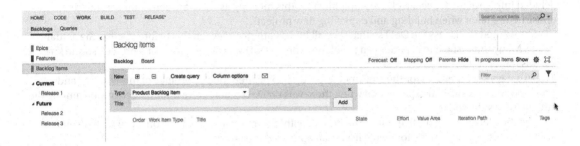

***Figure 8-17.** The Backlogs tab*

From the New Product Backlog Item field, she quickly created the first backlog item. She then opened the form shown in Figure 8-18 by double-clicking the first PBI.

***Figure 8-18.** The first PBI*

She took the first PBI on her backlog and started filling in the fields. She left a lot as it was for now and only filled in the PBI name and description. The area was Fabrikam Program Team and Iteration was the default.

Fiona then continued with the rest of the higher-level use cases until they were all in the TFS/VSTS. She often found stories that where epic-sized and they where entered as Epics, which she then broke down into features and then PBIs. Any PBI that she found could be associated with an epic or a feature was associated with that as a parent work item.

# Definition of Done (DoD)

Before going home that day, Fiona set up a date for a new meeting with the team to establish DoD. She included infrastructure specialist Dave Applemust for this meeting as there are constraints from the infrastructure team when building and deploying new projects.

She wanted to discuss the DoD so that they all had a common view on this before starting the actual coding. Many times she had experienced problems when a DoD was not in place for a project, so she knew this was important.

Two days later they met for the DoD meeting. Fiona explained the importance of this concept and spoke about issues she had experienced when there was no DoD. There were nods of recognition among the participants as she spoke.

She then let all of the participants write down the things they wanted to have on a DoD. After some discussion, they agreed on the following list for an approved user story:

- All code is written and checked in (including tests).

- Coding conventions are fulfilled (these are documented in a separate document and not included here).

- All unit tests must be passed (must be okayed before check-in).

- Code is to be refactored (improved/optimized without change of function).

- All code must be reviewed by at least two people (peer programming or peer review).

- The user story is included in the build (build scripts updated, all new modules included).

- The user story is installable (build scripts updated so that story is included in the automatic install).

- All acceptance tests are passed:

  - Acceptance criteria must exist.

  - Acceptance tests are implemented (automatic or manual tests) and test cases for them are created.

- Backlog is updated when:

  - All tasks have a remaining time equal to 0.

  - User story state is done.

  - Actual Hours is updated.

  - All tasks are done.

- User story is installed on the demoserver.

- User story is reviewed by the PO.

- User story is approved by the PO.

- Product documentation is updated and checked in.

- User manual is written.

- Administrative manual is updated.

- Help texts are written.

The team also came up with the following DoD for when the sprint is approved:

- All user stories in the sprint fulfill the DoD.
- Product is versioned (release management/rollback).
- All accepted bugs are corrected.
- New bugs that have been identified are closed or parked.
- Eighty percent code coverage from automated tests is fulfilled.
- All tasks are done and approved.
- All integration tests have passed.
- Sprint retrospective is performed and actions for improvements are identified.
- Sprint review, with PO present, has been performed.
- Performance test of the complete system has been done.

# Estimation

After establishing the DoD, they had what they needed to begin some initial estimation of the work. Fiona needed to come up with a rough budget for the project to show the stakeholders and also an initial release plan. She decided to use planning poker for this. She had used it previously and was happy with the result.

# Poker Planning/Story Points

They met in the same conference room. This time the entire team was there, not just the initial team. Fiona had purchased planning poker decks for everybody. She started by explaining the rules for everybody:

- Fiona started by reading the first user story.
- After a short time, each participant selected a card without showing it to the others.
- When Fiona asked them to show their cards, they turned them over.
- Cindy and Harry were the furthest apart. They both explained their thoughts on the user story and then the team played again.
- This time they were closer to each other's points (only one step apart) and the higher value was selected for the story.
- They continued through the user stories until they were finished.

# Updating the PBI

After they were done, Fiona went to her desk and started to update the PBIs. She now inserted the story points for each PBI into the work items in the Effort field. During sprint planning, these would be broken down into more manageable pieces and each task would get a time estimate instead of story points (Figure 8-19).

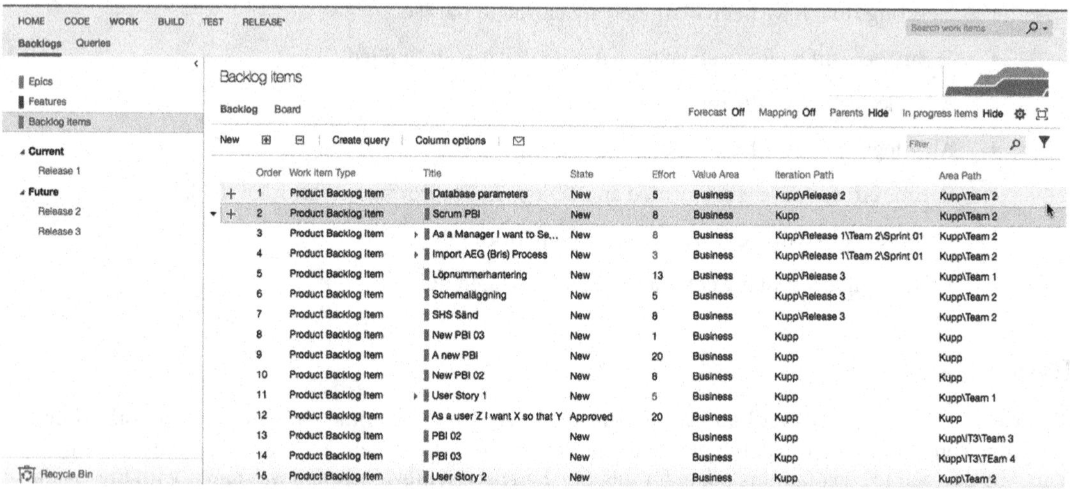

*Figure 8-19.* *Story points (effort) in the backlog*

So story points were now done, but before continuing to sprint planning and time estimates, Fiona wanted to perform an initial risk assessment.

# Risk Assessment

Risk assessment is part of all estimation in agile projects and should be done throughout the whole project. If any PBI is considered very risky, it might need to be prioritized higher on the backlog. It is always better to address high-risk items as early as possible to avoid surprises later. Fiona knew the surprises would come anyway.

There are different ways of performing risk assessments. We suggest you choose the one you are familiar with. Fiona chose to do a traditional risk assessment by using the following parameters:

- Severity (1-5)

- Probability (1-5)

- Risk

- Risk assessment score (severity × probability)

- Mitigations

- Probability after mitigation

- Risk assessment score after mitigation (severity × probability after mitigation)

They went through this analysis for each user story on the backlog. Fiona ended up with an Excel sheet like the one in Figure 8-20. Fiona checked this document into source control so everyone had access to it.

| User Story | Risk | Severity | Probability | Score | Mitigation | Probability after Mitigation | Score after Mitigation |
|---|---|---|---|---|---|---|---|
| As a Sales person I want to manage expense reports so that I can be more efficient | Expense reports cannot be created | 5 | 3 | 15 | Some Mitigation | 1 | 5 |
| As a Manager I want to Search Expense Reports so that I can | | | | | | | |

*Figure 8-20.* *Risk mitigation*

## Updating the Backlog Order

The team found no risks that were exceptional during the initial risk assessment, so Fiona left the backlog almost untouched. She only moved two stories a little higher in the list because the developers had recommended that she develop these a little earlier.

## Refining the Backlog

Throughout the sprints the PO needs to refine the backlog. The PO does not do this work alone, so the team needs to be part of this as well. This is an excellent way to get the team's views on the upcoming features and for them to give feedback and new ideas to the PO. Fiona decided to estimate about 10 percent of the team's time for backlog refinement. This number had worked well in the past.

Grooming the backlog also means that the PO has to order (prioritize) the backlog. Using TFS/VSTS, you can easily order the backlog by dragging a PBI up and down in the backlog view and thus change the order of that PBI.

---

■ **Note** A new feature in TFS/VSTS is the capability to tag PBIs. This way, you can get much finer granularity into how you organize your PBIs. You can use the tags any way you want; for instance, you can tag work items that are going to be included in a specific release with a tag for the release and so on.

---

# Initial Velocity

Fiona needed a few more things before she would arrive at the time estimates for the project. She needed to know the initial velocity of the team. The *velocity* is nothing more than the speed of the team. How much work (user stories) can they take on in a given sprint? She also needed to know how many hours they actually have for work in the sprints.

## Available Time

To calculate the available time for the team, Fiona used the following method:

- *How long is the sprint?* In this case, two weeks.

- *How many working days are available in the sprint?* Fiona would have ten working days.

- *How many days does each team member work during the sprint?* She needs to know planned vacation or other days off, planned meetings, and so on. She looked at each team member's schedule and filled in the numbers in TFS.

Fiona deducted the time for sprint planning, review, and retrospective meetings, which would be eight hours per person for this sprint. The TFS calculated the result of this. What you get is the capacity before drag. *Drag* is wasted time or unknown activities. Because the team was new and Fiona had not worked much with any of them, she used a standard 25 percent for the drag as she knew this could be a good landmark. Included in this is 10 percent backlog grooming. This usually results in six hours capacity per day (see Figure 8-21).

Now Fiona had the available number of hours in the sprint: 290.

## Capacity Planning in TFS

TFS is excellent to use for capacity planning. In the current sprint's backlog section, click the Capacity tab (Figure 8-21). Here you can set capacity, activities, and days out of office due to vacations and holidays. As you set capacity, activity, and days off, graphical information about hours and capacity is automatically generated in the pane on the right.

*Figure 8-21.  Entering capacity into TFS*

In Figure 8-22, you can see that in the current sprint (Sprint 1), the capacity is also shown in the Work Details tab in the far right and can be switched on or off.

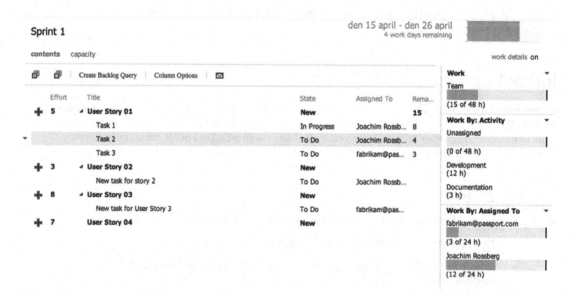

*Figure 8-22.  Viewing team capacity in sprint planning*

The sprint planning features in TFS offer three ways for the team to determine whether they have enough capacity: by person, by activity, or at the whole team level. This is very useful information for the product owner. You can see these estimations in the right panel in Figure 8-22 at the top under Team, which shows the collective work hours for the team. Below that you see Work By: Activity, showing the work that has been done so far in the Development and Documentation activities. You can also see Work By: Assigned To, which shows how much of each team member's capacity is assigned to tasks.

## Initial Sprint Planning

To calculate the initial velocity of the team, Fiona usually did an initial sprint planning. This is exactly the same as any sprint planning except that it is performed before the actual sprint starts. Fiona had in previous projects used this sprint planning in the first sprint because the two sprint planning meetings would be very similar and it would be unnecessary to perform it again.

During this meeting, the team estimates the tasks in hours so they can plan the sprint and decide on how many user stories they can take on in their sprint. This is the way the Fabrikam team performed this:

- Estimate the first user story in detail.

- Break down what the team needs to do to deliver the story.

- Estimate hours for each activity and summarize.

- Deduct the summary from the available time the team has in the sprint.

- Is there still time left? Take a new user story and repeat the process until no available time is left.

- Summarize the number of story points from the stories that were included in the sprint. That's the theoretical velocity.

The first (highest prioritized) user story on the backlog was:

*As a sales person I want to manage expense reports so I can be more efficient.*

The number of story points for this was five in the planning poker session. These was broken down into smaller tasks:

- Create expense report

- Delete expense report

- Modify expense report

- Send expense report for approval

- Log on to expense report system

Together with the team, Fiona prioritized these tasks so they had a beginning for the sprint backlog. The sprint backlog looked like this after prioritization:

- Create expense report

- Send expense report for approval

- Modify expense report

- Delete expense report

- Log on to expense report system

They continued breaking each of these down into smaller pieces and estimated them in hours. For creating the expense report, they came up with the following tasks:

- Create the graphical user interface (GUI)

- Create business logic

- Fulfill DoD requirement

- Write user manual

The estimated number of hours for this user story was 137. With an available time of 290 hours, they still had 153 left in the sprint. This meant that they still had room for more work, so they continued with the next user story on the backlog. This was:

*As a controller I want to be able to manage the users in the system so I have full control over the users.*

This was worth three story points.

After breaking this down, they had 95.5 hours left so they continued with another user story worth two story points. When this planning was done there remained 23.5 hours of available time, but Fiona and the team chose not to take on anything more in the sprint. The team was new and if there were problems, they wanted some space. It's better to finish all the tasks than to reach the end of the sprint and not be able to finish. If the team had time left in the sprint, they could take on more tasks, but they left that to decide later.

The total amount of story points for the sprint was now ten. This is the team's initial velocity. The sprint backlog now looked like this:

- Create expense report

- Send expense report for approval

- Modify expense report

- Delete expense report

- Log on to expense report system

- Create user

- Modify user

- Delete user

- Create customer

- Modify customer

- Delete customer

Each of these had tasks associated with them that are part of the complete sprint backlog.

## Updating Backlog and PBI

Throughout the sprint planning, Fiona updated the sprint backlog and inserted the new tasks into the TFS. She associated them with the first sprint for each team using the drop-down control (Figure 8-23). She also added the date when the first sprint would start under Manage Schedule and Iterations so that TFS was updated with this information.

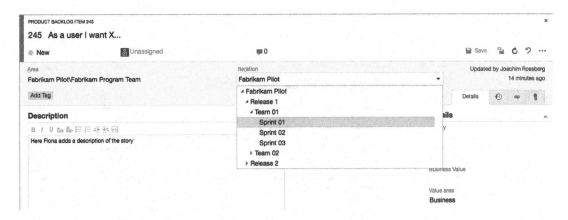

**Figure 8-23.** *Associating tasks with the sprint*

One thing worth considering here is what to do with the epic user stories in the backlog after they have been broken down. Are they still valid in the backlog at that point? In my opinion, you can safely remove these backlog items (by setting their status to Removed) as long as you are certain that the content is covered in the broken-down tasks. But this is a matter of how you want to work. Some people want to keep the epics, some don't. Microsoft says the Removed state is used "when the team will not implement the backlog item because product requirements or other work conditions have changed." But as stated earlier, this is a matter of how you want to work. Fiona kept the epics for reference. She got fine granularity of the backlog items at the top of the backlog and larger epics the further down the list she went. At this point, Fiona had a groomed backlog as well as a first sprint backlog.

---

■ **Note**    An *epic* is a large user story that is so big it is impossible to estimate how much effort it would take to develop it. It can also be a user story that is too large to fit into a single sprint, so it needs to be broken down. You can compare an epic to this user story:

As a human I would like to have world peace so that we humans will not kill one another anymore.

Although this example is farfetched, so are many epic user stories—at least until they are broken down into smaller, more manageable user stories.

---

## Forecast in TFS

There is a nice feature in TFS that will let you create a forecast on how much work you can have in each sprint. It requires that you fill in the effort estimate on each work item. The example in Figure 8-24 includes story points estimated in effort. You can see that forecasting is based on the velocity of five story points and TFS automatically draws the sprints and the work items that will fit into each sprint. The forecast can be switched off as well if you do not want to see it, simply by toggling on or off in the right top of the page.

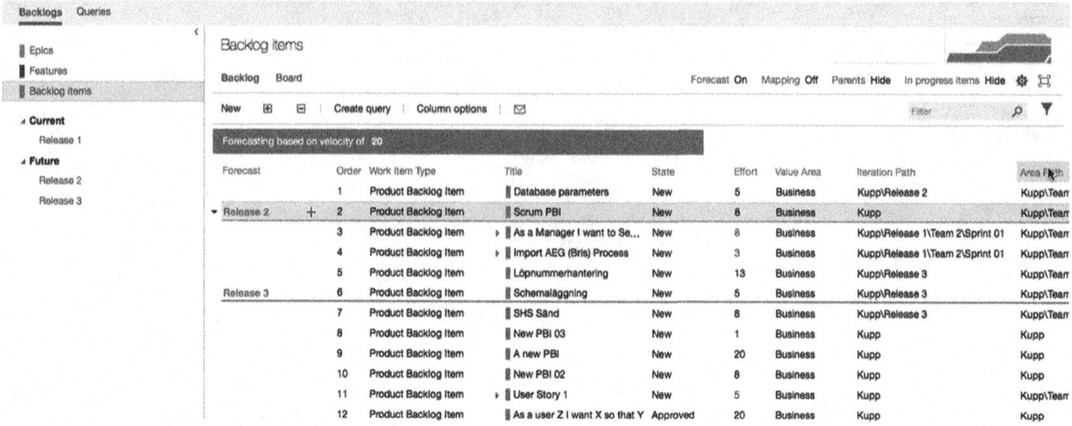

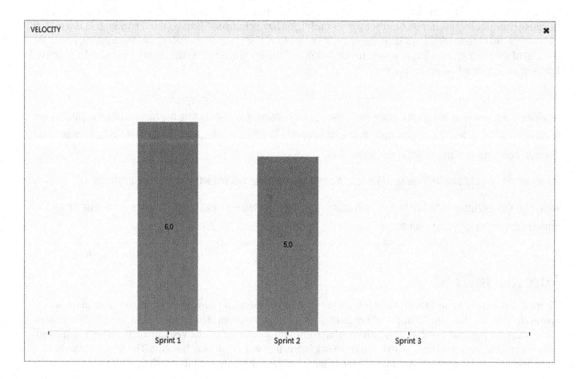

**Figure 8-24.** *Forecast in TFS*

You can use the Velocity report in the upper-right corner of the product backlog to view the historical velocity numbers, and, based on those numbers, determine a good velocity forecast number (Figure 8-25).

**Figure 8-25.** *Velocity report in web access*

You can also base a forecast on hours instead of story points; you simply change the values as you want.

# Release Planning

Based on the information she knew now, Fiona could start planning the releases of the project. She knew the management team would like to know how many releases were planned, and she wanted to give them this information as soon as she could. The first thing she did was look for epics (in the user stories) so she could come up with a release plan.

## Epics

Fiona looked at the backlog and came up with several epics:

- Expense report management
- Search functionality
- User management
- Customer management
- Project management
- Smartphone availability

She quickly saw that three epics were going to be part of the first sprint. According to the initial sprint planning, expense report management, user management, and customer management were all part of the first sprint.

Considering that there were many chores in the first sprint, she knew that it would not be possible to finish all three at the same time. She aimed at getting only the expense report management theme done in the first sprint. The other themes would come in the following sprints.

Fiona also knew the initial theoretical velocity (ten story points), which she used as an input for how much work she could expect in each sprint. With 44 story points total, the project would take 4.4 sprints to complete. She rounded this up to five sprints.

---

■ **Note**    A *chore* is just something a team needs to do. It could be setting up a build server, fixing the team room, fixing whiteboards, installing necessary software, and so on. Chores are never estimated. In the beginning, the first sprints are probably filled with chores just to get started. This means that the velocity in the first sprints will be lower than in the coming sprints when most chores are complete. There is just not as much room left for estimated work in the first sprints.

---

So, a rough overview would give the following release plan for the themes:

- Expense report management will be delivered in Sprint 1
- User management and customer management will be delivered in Sprint 2
- Project management and search management will be delivered in Sprint 3
- Smartphone availability will be delivered in Sprints 4 and 5, depending on smartphone type

## Estimated Time Plan

Fiona then used Excel to create a simple time plan for the project. She knew this was going to be temporary and could change depending on what happened during the project, so she would only show it to the stakeholders and not let them keep a copy of it.

# Estimated Project Cost

After this was completed, Fiona could come up with an initial estimate of the project cost. She knew how many weeks the project would take based on initial estimation, which was ten weeks. With the help of the administrative department, she could calculate the weekly cost of each of the team members. She then multiplied the weekly cost by the number of weeks and came up with a cost estimate. On top of this she added the hardware, software, and other costs she knew would appear. She arrived at an estimated project cost, which she used as input for the management meeting, where she would present the time plan and project budget. Luckily, the management team approved the project and she was good to go.

Fiona was now ready to start the project. She began by looking at the start-up dates, confirmed again with all managers of the team, and then sent out the invitation for the sprint planning meeting that would kick off Sprint 1. In the sprint planning meeting of Sprint 1, the team would use the initial sprint planning as explained in this chapter and see if anything had changed. If there had been changes, they might have to break down new user stories or change other aspects of the sprint. Hopefully, the initial sprint planning will remain the same as the actual Sprint 1 planning.

We have followed Fiona, the product owner, as she prepared the backlog for the first sprint. Fiona and the team have also done an initial sprint backlog planning to estimate an initial velocity. The team is now ready to jump into the first sprint. We will now leave Fiona and the team and talk more in general terms about how you can use TFS/VSTS during your sprints, based on the Scrum process template.

Before we take a look at how TFS/VSTS can help you run your sprints, let's take a brief look at the different meetings that take place during a sprint, as a refresher of the material covered in Chapter 3. This chapter uses the Microsoft Scrum template for all of the examples. If you use any other process template, you will see some differences.

# Scrum Meetings During the Sprint

During the sprint, you have several meetings that are included in the Scrum process:

- *Sprint planning*: At this meeting the development team, together with the product owner, selects user stories from the top of the backlog, breaks them down into tasks, and then estimates the tasks in hours.

- *Daily stand-up*: During the daily stand-up, which takes place at the same time every working day, the team members report what they have done since the last meeting, what they plan to do until the next meeting, and if they have any impediments.

- *Sprint review*: During the sprint review the team demonstrates the software they have built for the stakeholders and product owner. The results of the feedback from the participants can lead to new user stories, changes to user stories, or perhaps removal of user stories.

- *Sprint retrospective*: During the sprint retrospective, the team discusses what they have done well during the sprint, what was not so good, and what they can do to improve their process.

- *Backlog grooming*: Although not an official Scrum meeting, the backlog grooming is important. During this session the product owner and the team look at user stories for coming sprints (usually one or two sprints ahead) and estimate the stories in story points. The estimation occurs after the PO has explained what each story contains.

TFS/VSTS can help support these meetings in various ways during the sprint, so let's start by looking at the sprint planning.

## Sprint Planning

Most of the work at the sprint planning meeting will be to break down user stories into tasks and estimate the time for each task. The team starts with the top story from the product backlog, breaks it down, and places it on the sprint backlog. They continue doing this until the amount of available time for the sprint is full.

In TFS/VSTS, you can add tasks to a user story in a couple of different ways. From inside a PBI, you can go to the Links tab and click the Add Linked Work Item icon, as shown in Figure 8-26.

*Figure 8-26. Adding a new task from inside a user story*

This will open the form shown in Figure 8-27. Once the form is opened, you can add some basic information, such as a title and comments. When you are done with this, click OK to create the task.

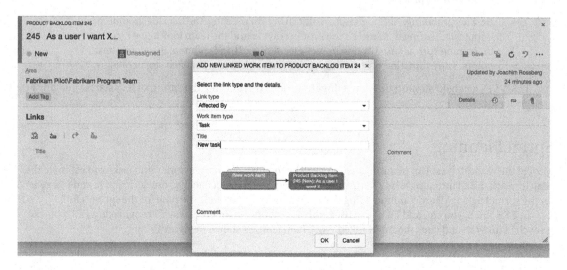

***Figure 8-27.*** *Add new task form*

Note that you cannot add any other work item this way. To link a user story (or other work item) to another work item type, you need to follow another workflow, which we will explain shortly. Clicking OK will open the task for more detailed editing, as shown in Figure 8-28.

***Figure 8-28.*** *Filling in additional information on a task*

During sprint planning, you can choose to assign the tasks right away or you can wait until all tasks for the sprint have been estimated. This depends entirely on how you want to work.

You can also fill in the description of what the task means, which is something you should not forget to do. We have seen many tasks without a good description, which causes confusion once work starts on the task. A good suggestion is to let the team decide on what information they want in a task to minimize wasting time.

One thing that we would say is mandatory is the Remaining Work field, which you will find in the Details section. It is important to register remaining work on a project and a common suggestion is to update this field at the end of every working day. This is the only field you can use in the process template for following up and estimating hours on a task. The burndown chart (Figure 8-29) uses this information to display how much total work time there is left for all tasks in the sprint. This will help you see a trend of when you can expect to be done with all of the tasks. You would have had to list all of the team members' capacity for the sprint in order for this to be correct.

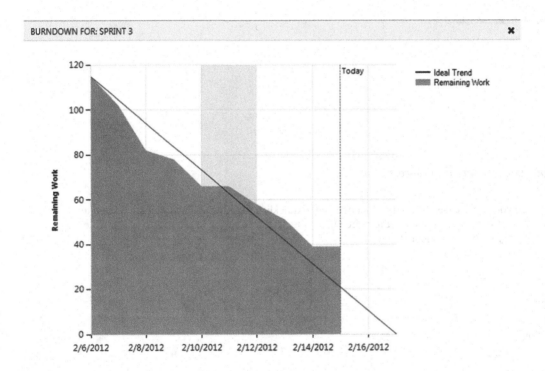

***Figure 8-29.*** *The burndown chart uses the remaining work field to calculate when the tasks in a sprint will be done*

You can also add information about what activity the task is connected to. Here you can define these activities yourself from the Control Panel, so this can be tailored to your own needs. The same goes for the Field area. Activity is often the field used for defining what part of the process a task belongs to, and Area is the field often used for functional or component breakdown, but you can use them as you see fit. This gives flexibility in how you can search and find tasks and other work items when you need to.

A new feature added in Visual Studio 2012 update 1 was tagging, which lets you tag a work item with one or more tags and then later filter the backlog using these tags. A *tag* is just a short text and you can define as many as you want.

As shown in Figure 8-30, we have created a tag on this backlog item that indicates that the work being done is related to integration.

*Figure 8-30. Adding tags to a work item*

Now you can use tags on the product backlog to quickly find only the items that are related to integration. Click the filter icon on the right edge of the product backlog to see the list of available tags for this backlog, as shown in Figure 8-31.

*Figure 8-31. Tag filter*

Note that each tag also shows the number of work items on the current backlog that have this tag. You can click a tag to filter the backlog to only show the items with the corresponding tag.

As with any other work item, you can also add attachments and links to a task. Attachments (Figure 8-32) can be of any kind: documents, figures, and what have you.

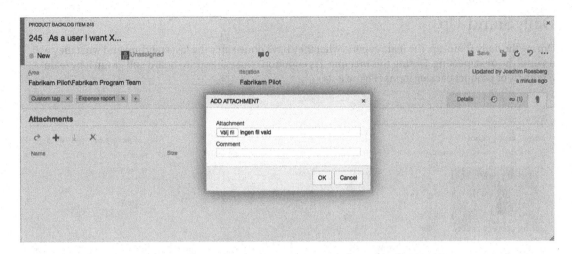

***Figure 8-32.*** *Adding attachments to a work item*

If you want to use the board to create a task, you can do so by clicking the plus sign (Figure 8-33) at the top-right corner of a user story. You will then be directed to the same workflow as described previously.

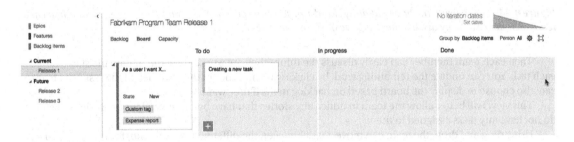

***Figure 8-33.*** *Creating a new task from the board view*

All of these possibilities—breaking down backlog items into tasks, linking to attachments, and creating other work items in conjunction with the tags field, area, activity, remaining work, and so on—are essential to have during sprint planning. During this meeting you can find new user stories that need to be added or impediments you need to create.

Because test cases are included in the things you can create and link to tasks and user stories, testers can also benefit from the TFS/VSTS features during sprint planning. Depending on how testers want to work, they can create test cases and link them directly to a product backlog item. In one recent project, the tester used the acceptance criteria in the product backlog item to create test cases, linking them directly to the product backlog item.

# Daily Stand-Up

During the daily stand-up, the team reports what they have done since the last stand-up and what they will do until the next meeting. During this meeting it is common to use the sprint board and group it by team members or product backlog items (Figure 8-34).

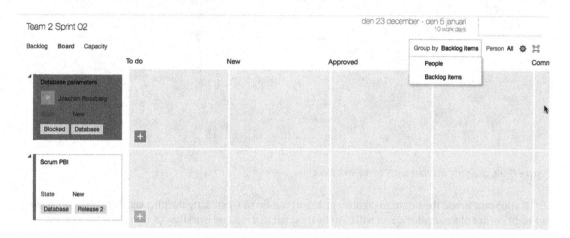

***Figure 8-34.*** *When using the board at daily stand-up, you can sort the board on team members and then each team member can easily discuss the things he or she is working on*

Then each team member can easily discuss the things they are working on and update the status of each task. You can update the remaining work by clicking the number in the lower left of the task. The team can also choose to display the board based on backlog items if they want.

This view will better allow the team to notice any stories that have been selected for the sprint but still do not have any tasks assigned to them.

Using drag and drop, the team can move a task between the different columns and, for instance, move a task to done when it is ready as defined in the definition of done. This feature also allows you to quickly move a task between team members so you do not have to open the task and select a new assignee—really useful in our opinion!

---

▓ **Note**  The board is based on tasks only. We do not show user stories in the columns. If you want a board for user stories, you can use the Kanban board.

---

At the daily stand-up, the team also discusses any impediments they might have. Using the linking features described here, you can create and link an impediment (Figure 8-35) to a task or user story and assign the impediment to the correct person. You can also select a priority (between 1 and 4) if you want.

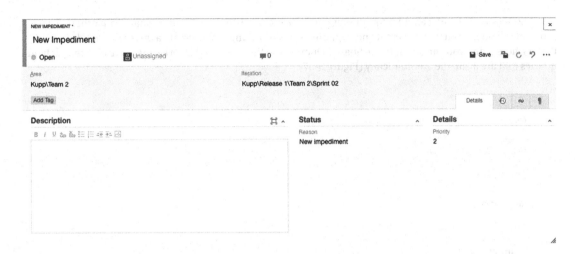

**Figure 8-35.** *Impediments work item type form*

# Retrieving Data from TFS/VSTS

If you navigate to the Work Items tab on the team's web portal, you have some options of getting information from TFS/VSTS that can be useful during the sprints.

The Query tab by default shows all work items that have been assigned to an individual (Figure 8-36). If you take a look at the left menu, you see queries that will give more information about the status of your projects. You can see that you can add queries to My Favorites, which will be useful if you quickly want to find a specific query. You can also see that you have some Team Favorites, where you can add queries that will be accessible to the whole team.

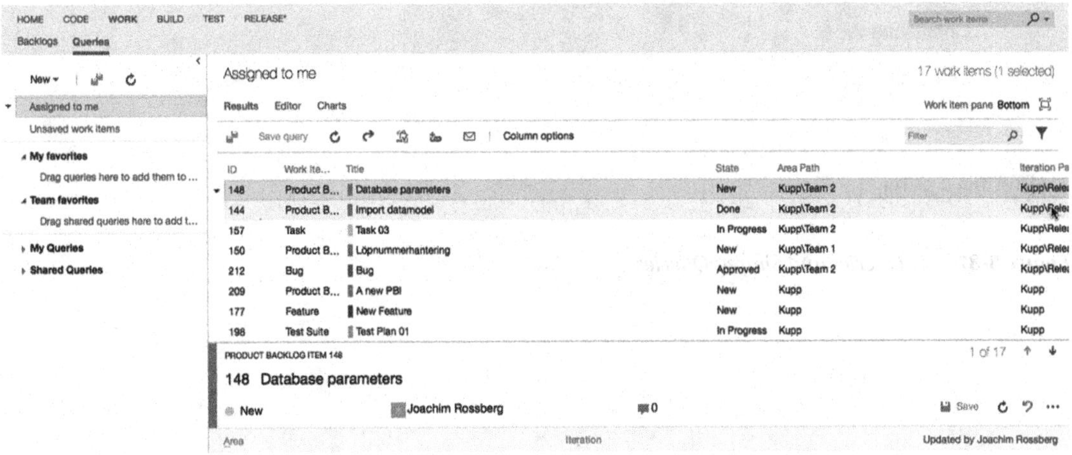

**Figure 8-36.** *Query view shows what has been assigned to me*

My Queries is the placeholder for queries you have created but do not want to share with others. There is no default query, but you can create new queries as you go along. If you create a query that will be useful to the whole team, you can add it to the Shared Queries list. Below Shared Queries there are different default queries that are available automatically (Figure 8-37).

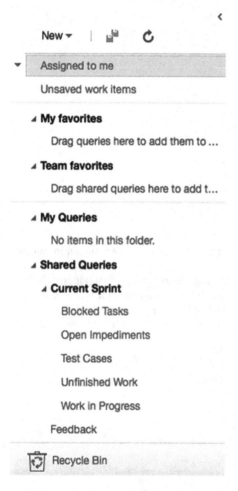

*Figure 8-37.* *My Queries and Shared Queries*

Running a query results in a list with the work items affected by the query. Figure 8-38 shows the results from the Open Impediments query.

**Figure 8-38.** *Query result from the Open Impediments query*

If you want to go into a query and edit it, you can do so by clicking the Editor link. That way you can modify the query or create a new one.

These shared queries are very useful to many team members. The PO can retrieve status information from TFS/VSTS regarding the project and the project health. The team members can quickly find work items that are connected to them so they can keep track of what work is at hand.

# Backlog Refinement

As was explained earlier, the PO needs to refine the backlog during the sprint so it is in good shape. This means that the backlog should be ordered and that the top backlog items should be broken down into smaller, more manageable pieces. The team helps the PO with this, and we estimate roughly 10 percent of available time for the team for this task.

The PO updates the TFS/VSTS backlog so it reflects reality. There might be new user stories that must be added, modifications to others, and so on. You can easily drag and drop items on the backlog to change the order, which is a nice feature.

# Sprint Review

The sprint review is the meeting where the team shows the PO and any other stakeholder(s) what they have built during the sprint. Any working software should be demoed so that the PO can sign off on the user stories that have been delivered. Nothing of what is shown should be a surprise to the PO. He or she should have been a continual part of the sprint so there should be no surprises here.

In the sprint review meeting, the team can look at the sprint backlog to verify that all backlog items that were worked on and marked as complete are covered in the review.

## Sprint Retrospective

During the retrospective, you look at what was good and what was bad during the sprint. This is by far the most important meeting in Scrum. Why? Because this is where you learn how to improve. Constant retrospective and adaptation is essential for the team if they are to deliver quality software and business value.

This meeting helps you discover what needs to change in the way you run your meetings, for example. You can also determine whether there is a problem with communication with the PO or another part of the organization. This input is valuable so that you can change the way your teams work in order to achieve even better results during the next sprint.

We usually execute the sprint retrospective by using a white piece of paper and dividing it with a marker pen. The left side is for what was good (marked by a +) and the right side is for what was not good (marked by a -). The team then calls out what their opinions are and the Scrum master documents this on the paper. Sometimes very specific issues such as writing better comments during check-in are listed, but there can also be softer issues such as "improve communications in the team."

Another way to run this meeting is to answer three questions:

- What should we stop doing?
- What should we start doing?
- What should we continue doing?

The answers to these questions will provide great input to your continuous improvement process. Both of the described methods work very well. Use a method that works for your team; the important thing is that you perform the meeting and take the opportunity to adapt from the results.

Based on this retrospective, the Scrum master and the team select a few issues from the bad side and commit to improve these. Issues that need to be taken care of are documented as tasks or impediments in TFS/VSTS so that you can follow up on them and assign them to the correct person.

# Summary

This chapter followed Fiona on her project for Fabrikam Fiber. You saw how she initiated the project and started to use VSTS to run it once it was given the go. In this chapter Fiona used VSTS but she could also have been using an on-premise TFS.

You saw how you can use various aspects of the TFS/VSTS product to manage an agile project. This concludes this book. I hope you have enjoyed it.

# Index

## A

Agile management
  acceptance criteria, 118
  alert management
    alert selection, 162–163
    backlog building, 165, 169
    DoD, 166
    PBI, 168
    poker planning/story points, 167
    requirements, 163
    risk assessment, 168
  architecture, analysis and design, 136
  automated testing, 123
  code-analysis warnings, 137–138
  code coverage, 137
  code metrics, 137
  code refactoring, 128
  coding standard, 128
  continuous delivery, 118, 127
  continuous integration, 118, 125
  cost estimation, 176
  errors and warnings, 137
  Fabrikam development manager, 147
  initial velocity
    available time, 169
    backlog updation, 172
    capacity planning, 170
    forecast, 173
    initial sprint planning, 172
    PBI, 172
  monitoring, 145
  MTM, 121
  pair programming, 129
  pilot project, 148
  project management metrics, 134
    backlog overview report, 131–132
    burn rate chart, 132–133
    sprint burndown report, 131–132
    unplanned work report, 132, 135
    velocity report, 134

  project release planning, 175
  project startup phase
    bugs creation, 152
    team building, 153
  regression testing, 117
  release management, 143
  Scrum process
    backlog refinement, 177, 185
    charts, 150
    daily stand-up, 176, 182
    queries, 150, 185
    sprint planning, 176, 181
    sprint retrospective, 177, 186
    sprint review, 176
    TFS/VSTS web portal, 149
  TDD, 122
  team creation
    area path, 154
    backlog structure, 157
    iteration structure, 157
    members, 159
    Project Profile page, 155
    team building, 158
    values, 155–156
    web access page, 154
  test proportion, 119–120
  VSTS group, 161
  WTM, 121
Application lifecycle management (ALM), 65
  ALM 1.0, 12
  ALM 2.0, 15
  ALM 2.0+, 17
  APM view, 4, 6
  aspects, 1
  collaboration, 20
  DevOps, 17
  high-level processes, automation, 8, 19
  IT and business, 20
  process automation, 9
  SDLC view, 4–5
  Serena Software, 9–10

© Joachim Rossberg 2016
J. Rossberg, *Agile Project Management using Team Foundation Server 2015*,
DOI 10.1007/978-1-4842-1870-9

Application lifecycle management (ALM) (*cont.*)
  service management/operations view, 4, 6
  switching, 20
  tasks, 63
  team planning, 64
  test artifacts, 64
  tools, 63
  traceability, 8, 19
  unified view, 4, 7
  visibility, 9, 19
Application Portfolio Management (APM), 4, 6

## ■ B

Backlog grooming, 15
Backlog refinement, 185

## ■ C

Capability Maturity Model
        Integration (CMMI), 76, 80
Concurrent Versions System (CVS), 14
Continuous integration (CI), 125

## ■ D

Defined process control, 38
Definition of Done (DoD), 166

## ■ E, F, G, H

Empirical process control, 39
Extreme Programming (XP), 58

## ■ I, J

Integrated Development Environment (IDE), 24
Iterations, 40

## ■ K, L

Kanban method
  continuous, incremental, and
        evolutionary change, 54
  models, 57
  operations, 53
  principles, 54
  process policy, 57
  roles, responsibilities, and job titles, 54
  scientific method, 57
  WIP limit, 56
  workflow management, 56
  workflow visualization, 54–55
Key performance indicator (KPI). *See* Agile
        management

## ■ M

Microsoft Test Manager (MTM), 120

## ■ N

Nexus, 61–63

## ■ O

Ordering the backlog, 50

## ■ P, Q, R

Planning poker, 49
Process customization
  areas and iterations, 93
  process template XML file, 89
  reports, 92
  Team Explorer, 96
  VSTS, 110, 115
    agile process, 112
    attributes, 111
    Create Process, 109
    field view, 114
    process configuration, 106–107
  web access
    backlog, 105–106
    bugs, 103
    color-code tags, 104
    column configuration, 104–105
    Kanban board, 102–103
  workflow, 101
  work items, 112–113
    field, 99
    queries, 91
    types, 90

## ■ S

Scaled Agile Framework (SAFe), 61
Scaled Professional Scrum (SPS), 61
Scrum, 76, 78
  approaches, 37
  backlog, 51, 177, 185
  charts, 150
  complexity-assessment graph, 39
  daily stand-up, 176, 182
  definition, 38
  DoD, 47
  empirical process control, 39
  estimation, 50
  iterations, 41
  process of

functional and non-functional
    requirements, 43
sprint planning meeting, 44–45
product owner, 42
queries, 150, 185
scaling, 59
Scrum master, 43
sprint planning meeting
    daily stand-ups, 51, 176, 181
    sprint retrospective, 52, 177, 186
    sprint review, 52, 176
team, 42
TFS/VSTS web portal, 149
user stories, 48
Software development lifecycle (SDLC), 1, 4–5
Story points, 49
Support Microsoft Test Manager (MTM), 84

## T, U

Team Foundation Server (TFS)
    agilemanagement (see Agile management)
    CMMI, 76, 81
    collaboration
        IT and business, 33
        reports and queries, 31
        team room, 31–32
        work items, 32
    extensibility, 34
    high-level processes, automation, 29
    IDE, 24
    processcustomization (see Process
        customization)
    process template, 22
    Scrumprocess (see Scrum)
    support MTM, 85

traceability
    configuration management, 28
    executable system, 75
    features, 25
    Microsoft Office SharePoint Server, 24, 66
    queries, 74
    rescue team, 66
    tools, 67
    user story, 74
    work items, 26, 70
visibility, 30
Visual Studio Team Services, 21, 23, 34
web access, 24
workflow states, 83
Team velocity, 50
Test-driven development (TDD), 122

## V

Visual Studio Team Services (VSTS), 110, 115
    agile process, 112
    attributes, 111
    Create Process, 109
    field view, 114
    process configuration, 106–107
    Scrum process, 149
    vs. TFS
    work item type, 112–113

## W, X, Y, Z

Web Test Case Manager (WTM), 121
Windows Communication
        Foundation (WCF), 14
Windows Presentation Services, 14
Work in Process (WIP) limit, 56

# Get the eBook for only $5!

Why limit yourself?

Now you can take the weightless companion with you wherever you go and access your content on your PC, phone, tablet, or reader.

Since you've purchased this print book, we're happy to offer you the eBook in all 3 formats for just $5.

Convenient and fully searchable, the PDF version enables you to easily find and copy code—or perform examples by quickly toggling between instructions and applications. The MOBI format is ideal for your Kindle, while the ePUB can be utilized on a variety of mobile devices.

To learn more, go to www.apress.com/companion or contact support@apress.com.

Printed in the United States
By Bookmasters